FOREWORD

Theodore Ziolkowski

PHILOSOPHER, novelist, poet, essayist, dramatist—the multifaceted Unamuno was
the undisputed intellectual leader of the brilliant
Generation of '98 that ushered in a second golden
age of Spanish culture. Together with the essayist
Azorín, the novelist Pío Baroja, the political theo-
rist Ramiro de Maeztu, and the poet Antonio
Machado, he fought for the cultural renewal of a
Spain that, through the humiliating loss of Cuba
and the Philippines in the Spanish-American War,
had been deprived of the last vestiges of its one-
time glory and was mired in intellectual provincial-
ism and spiritual decline. Yet he soon parted com-
pany with those of his contemporaries who believed
that Spain must Europeanize itself in order to catch
up with the rest of the Western world on the eve of
the twentieth century. With his characteristic intran-
sigence matching the stone and bronze of the three
statues commemorating him in Salamanca, he insisted in his fierce national pride and his hostility to
science and rationalism that Europe must be
"Hispanized" by the spirit of Don Quixote.
    Unamuno's life and thought reveal a jumble of

contradictions that might have destroyed a lesser man. A proud Basque who came to exemplify Spanish culture, a modern existentialist who claimed a medieval soul, a professor and university rector contemptuous of the specialized scholarship that he called "a form of mental laziness," a prolific novelist best remembered for his antinovels overturning all fictional conventions, a happily married father of nine children who was obsessed by the tragicomedy of sexual love, a cultural nationalist who studied German by deciphering Hegel and learned Danish in order to read Kierkegaard, Unamuno was fond of quoting Walt Whitman: "Do I contradict myself? / Very well then, I contradict myself. / (I am large, I contain multitudes)."

Born into a strictly Catholic middle-class family in Bilbao in 1864, Miguel de Unamuno y Jugo experienced the contradictions of life while still a schoolboy when he was torn between the mystical longing to become a priest and his more earthly love for the girl who was to become his wife. At the University of Madrid, exposed to a world of new ideas that challenged the unquestioning faith of his childhood, he studied modern philosophy along with Greek antiquity and wrote a dissertation on the origins and prehistory of the Basques. Returning to Bilbao in 1884, he prepared for qualification as a university professor but failed successively to win the chairs for which he applied in Basque, logic, metaphysics, and Latin. Finally in 1891, the year of his marriage, he was awarded the chair of Greek language at the ancient University of Salamanca, where he was to spend the rest of his life teaching Greek (although he never wrote a word on classical philology) and, later, the history of the Spanish language. It was here, in 1897, that he underwent a profound spiritual crisis, precipitated by the fatal illness of a child, that led him to the religious psychology of William James and, most important, to Kierkegaard's attacks on institutionalized Christianity.

In 1900, despite the combativeness exemplified by the aggressive thrust of his pointed beard, Unamuno was appointed rector of his university, a position that he held until 1914, when he was dismissed without explanation. During those enormously productive years he established himself as the leading Spanish intellectual and cultural critic of his day and wrote the two works for which he remains best known: the philosophical essays published under the title *The Tragic Sense of Life* (1913) and the "novel" *Mist* (1914).

Temperamentally anarchic and incapable of systematic philosophy, Unamuno followed the model of Nietzsche and Kierkegaard, together with whom he can be seen to constitute a powerful triumvirate of pre-existential thinkers, addressing the general public in essayistic reflections written in a passionately compelling language. What defines humanity is the consciousness lacking in the world of nature. Yet inherent in that very consciousness is, for Unamuno, the tragedy of life. Like the Underground Man of Dostoevsky, to whom he felt spiritually akin, Unamuno begins with the premise that "consciousness is a disease." Living and knowing are such antinomies that "everything vital is, not only irrational, but anti-rational, and everything rational is anti-vital." The consciousness that distinguishes us from, say, the ant or the sun and that arouses in us "the appetite to know for the sole pleasure of knowing" at the same time alerts us to our existence and awakens within us what Unamuno calls "The Hunger for Immortality." Indeed, his preoccupation with death is matched in modern philosophy only by that of Heidegger, who (in a conversation with the Hispanist M. J. Valdés) acknowledged his debt to Unamuno. It is the desire for personal immortality that produces love, "the most tragic thing there is." Sexual love, through which we seek to perpetuate ourselves, turns out to be a battle of mutual egotisms. "Each of the lovers is, for the other, an immediate instrument of enjoyment and a mediate instrument of perpetuation."

In the concluding essay on "Don Quixote in the Contemporary European Tragicomedy" Unamuno returns to the figure that dominates his imagination and provides the exemplary model for the fundamental tragedy of modern Spain: the conflict between reality and imagination or between science and religion. "I feel within me a medieval soul," Unamuno confesses, "and I feel that my country's soul is also medieval, that this soul has perforce lived through the Renaissance, the Reformation, and the Revolution, learning from them, certainly, but never allowing the essence of the soul to be changed, always preserving intact the spiritual inheritance derived from the so-called Dark Ages. And Quixotism is simply the most desperate phase of the battle of the Middle Ages against its offspring the Renaissance" (translated by Anthony Kerrigan). Don Quixote tilting against the windmill exemplifies for Unamuno his own idealistic battle against modern technology and rationalism.

Mist (*Niebla*) is the fictional exemplification of these ideas. Anticipating later writers such as Albert Camus and Jean-Paul Sartre, Unamuno exploited fiction as a vehicle for the exploration of philosophical themes. Fiction provides an appropriate mode for philosophical experimentation, because, as he observes in the first chapter of *The Tragic Sense of Life,* Unamuno is concerned not with such abstract ideas as "mankind" or "humanity" but with the reality of "The Man of Flesh and Blood." Rejecting the generic term *novel* as being tied to modern notions of realism and reason,

Unamuno coined the term *nivola* (a phonetic amalgam of *novela* and *niebla*) to designate the new kind of fiction that he was henceforth to write: antinovels that shatter conventional illusions of reality and treat fictionality ironically. The nivola, as his work is designated in the subtitle of the Spanish original, dispenses almost wholly with the norms of the nineteenth-century realistic novel—notably action, description of time and place, and analysis of character—and depends entirely on dialogue revealing the struggles of what Unamuno called his "agonists." In the theory of the nivola outlined in chapter 17 of the novel, Unamuno even states that the nivola has no plot: the characters take over the action, and the author becomes "the plaything of his own inventions."

This play with fictional conventions and with various levels of reality is evident in the two prologues. One is purportedly written by Victor Goti, who turns out to be a character within Unamuno's nivola, and the other by Unamuno himself, who takes issue with the views of his invented character. The playfulness continues to the last pages of the work, which record the "funeral oration" of the dog Orfeo, who dies of sadness following his master's death. (The talking dog is a staple in European literature, from Lucian's satirical dialogues down to Kafka's *Investigations of a Dog* or Bulgakov's *Heart of a Dog*, but Unamuno is no doubt indebted specifically to the famous model of Cervantes' *Dogs' Colloquy*.)

The central metaphor suggested by the title is likewise a modern variation of a theme dear to Spanish literature of the Golden Age: *La vida es sueño*. But instead of the "dream" in Calderón's formulation, life is for the "agonist" of Unamuno's antinovel a nebula, a mist resembling the snow that obscures all contours in Kafka's *The Castle* or the foggy swamps of Gide's *Paludes*. When Augusto Pérez, a precursor of the antiheroes of Sartre's *Nausea* and *The Stranger* by Camus, first appears at the door of his house, he is totally alienated from reality. The pampered son of a recently deceased mother, he leads a meaningless existence conditioned almost entirely by the mists of habit. So ritualistic is his behavior that he is incapable of deciding whether to walk to the right or the left and therefore waits for a dog, or a person, to pass his doorstep so that he can follow. On the morning when the nivola begins, it is Eugenia, a pretty young piano teacher who dislikes music, who awakens Augusto from his somnambulistic existence, arousing him to consciousness and action.

To be sure, it is not the "real" Eugenia, a deceitful schemer, who attracts Augusto, but rather his idealizing image of her, based almost wholly on his impression of her eyes. Indeed, her affairs have achieved a certain notoriety in the town, known to everyone but Augusto, who is so obsessed with his image of her that he repeatedly fails to notice the woman herself when he passes her in the street. His story is in one sense an expanded version of the anecdote that Augusto recounts concerning the Portuguese fireworks-maker who was blinded in an explosion that also destroyed his wife's vaunted beauty; so vivid was the image of her beauty in his mind, however, that he continued to boast about it for years to come while his friends, out of sympathy, went along with his self-deception.

The "cynical" comment upon the Quixotic obsession with inner visions that is blind to reality is expressed in the epilogue by the dog Orfeo, who notes that human beings are made miserable by the fact of their consciousness and their incessant chatter, which deprives them of natural health and contentedness. "As soon as he gives a thing a name he ceases to see the thing itself; he only hears the name that he gave it or sees it written. His language enables him to falsify, to invent what does not exist, and to confuse himself. For him everything in the world is merely a pretext for talking to other men or far talking to himself."

The most powerful result of consciousness is the desire for immortality through sexual love. Augusto's dormant sense of womankind is stirred by Eugenia, as he puts it, from the abstract to the concrete and then to the generic. The "action" of

the nivola, such as it is, amounts to often cynical
variations on the theme of love and marriage. Au-
gustus is betrayed by Eugenia, who goes off at his
expense with her lover Mauricio. The laundress
Rosario, at one time the lover of Mauricio, is in
turn betrayed by Augusto. Augusto's friend Victor
Goti is forced into a shotgun marriage because his
girlfriend is thought to be pregnant; when the
pregnancy turns out to be false, they try for years
to have a child until they become accustomed to
their carefree childlessness. As a result, when after
twelve years of childless marriage Victor's wife
finally does become pregnant, they regard the future offspring only as "the intruder" until, in an
unexpected twist, they become attached to the new
son. In another episode, Don Antonio's wife leaves
him for another man, and Don Antonio resolves to
take care of the man's deserted wife and child. Although they cannot marry, they have four children
and live happily together outside the bonds of matrimony.

If *Mist* amounts to a fictional commentary on
the tragic sense of life arising from consciousness
and the hunger for immortality, its most famous
scene seeks to make readers forget that they are
reading a fictional account and, if only for a passing moment, doubt their own reality. In his reflections on *The Life of Don Quixote and Sancho*
(1905), Unamuno had claimed that although we

sometimes regard writers as real persons and regard the characters they invent as purely imaginary, the truth is exactly the reverse. "The characters are real, it is they who are the authentic beings, and they make use of the person who seems to be of flesh and blood in order to assume form and being in the eyes of men." Unamuno makes the serious assertion that Don Quixote and Sancho Panza have more historical reality than Cervantes himself and that "far from Cervantes being their creator, it is they who created Cervantes." In *Mist,* Unamuno puts this theory into action.

Exhausted and depressed by Eugenia's betrayal and by the incoherence of existence, Augusto decides to kill himself and thus extinguish the consciousness that is the cause of his misery. Before doing so, he journeys to Salamanca to consult the philosopher Unamuno and to get his views on suicide. During the course of their conversation, however, Unamuno points out to Augusto that he does not have the luxury of taking his life, because he exists only as a fictitious entity. "You are only a product of my imagination and of the imagination of those of my readers who read this story which I have written of your fictitious adventures and misfortunes." Initially distraught at this revelation, Augusto regains his composure and goes on the attack. Reminding Unamuno that he has repeatedly argued that Don Quixote and Sancho are more real

than Cervantes himself, Augusto suggests that it is
Unamuno and not he who is the fictitious entity.
"May it not be that you are nothing more than a
pretext for bringing my history into the world?"

The nivola ends ambiguously: Augusto goes
back home and dies of a heart attack after eating
himself almost to death; it remains uncertain
whether he has succeeded in committing suicide or
whether his author has taken his life. However that
may be, Unamuno created—a decade before Piran-
dello in *Six Characters in Search of an Author*—the
classic source for the interplay of fiction and reality that has become a staple of postmodern fiction
and philosophy. In Kurt Vonnegut's *Breakfast of
Champions* the author sits with his character,
Kilgore Trout, in the cocktail lounge of a Holiday
Inn and informs him that he is a novelist who has
invented Trout for use in his books. In John
Barth's *Letters* the author writes to figures from his
earlier novels to solicit their cooperation as characters in a new work of fiction. In Jostein Gaarder's
international bestseller *Sophie's World,* Sophie and
another character, having become aware of their
fictionality, decide to liberate themselves from the
novel by slipping away while their author's attention is distracted. One of Unamuno's greatest ad-
mirers has suggested an explanation for the unset-
tling effect of this play with fiction and reality. In
his essay on *Don Quixote* Jorge Luis Borges wrote:

"These inversions suggest that if the characters of a fictional work can be readers or spectators, we, its readers or spectators, can be fictitious." It is because of the implicit frangibility of our consciousness that the shifting boundary of literature and life produces the ambiguous effect of weird amusement and existential anxiety in its readers.

Following his unexplained removal from the rectorship in 1914, Unamuno continued to teach while writing further philosophical essays and a succession of experimental nivolas, including *Abel Sanchez, Three Exemplary Novels,* and *How a Novel Is Made.* In 1920 he accepted the position of vice-rector, which he held until 1924, when his political disagreements with Primo de Rivera resulted in his deportation to the Canary Islands. Fleeing to France, Unamuno spent the following six years in exile until the fall of the dictatorship enabled him to return to Spain, where, in 1931, he was reappointed rector. In 1934, at age seventy, he stopped lecturing but continued to serve as rector until new political disagreements, this time with the Republic, caused his dismissal in 1936. Later that year he was restored to the rectorship, only to be relieved of it yet again. Confined to his home in Salamanca, this towering figure of political, philosophical, and literary controversy died on the last day of 1936. In the vast and varied body of his work, none conveys his intellectual legacy more effectively than *Mist,* in which we acknowledge both a monument of the philosophical novel and a chef d'oeuvre of modern experimental fiction.

MIST

PROLOGUE

Don Miguel de Unamuno insists upon my writing a prologue for this book of his in which he tells the sad story of my good friend Augusto Pérez and of his strange death; and since the wishes of Señor Unamuno are for me commands, in the most genuine sense of the word, I can do no less than write it. Without having reached the extreme of Hamletian scepticism attained by my poor friend Pérez, who came to the point of doubting his own existence, I am at least firmly persuaded that I lack what the psychologists call free will, though I am also consoled by the belief that Don Miguel enjoys just as little of it as I.

It will doubtless seem strange to some readers that I, who am quite unknown in the Spanish republic of letters, should be the one to write the prologue of a book by Don Miguel, who is already favourably known there; since it is the custom in prologues for the better known writers to introduce others who are less known. But Don Miguel and I have formed an agreement to change this pernicious custom, reversing the terms so that the unknown shall introduce the known. For the fact is *that books are bought more for the text than for the prologue; and therefore it is not a bad idea that when a young man like me wishes to make himself known, instead of asking a veteran of letters to write him a prologue of introduction, he should ask his permission to put a prologue of his own into one of that writer's works. And this at the same time solves one of the problems involved in that eternal dispute between young and old.*

I am united to Don Miguel de Unamuno by not a few ties. Apart from what this Señor brings to light in the book, be it a novel or a "nivola"
*— and note that the "*nivola*" is my own invention*
— I had many long conversations with the unfortunate Augusto Pérez; and apart also from the fact that in the novel Don Miguel tells the story of the rather tardy birth of my son Victorcito, it seems that I am related to him by distant bonds of blood, indeed that my surname is that of one of Don Miguel's ancestors, as I gather from the learned genealogical investigations conducted by my friend Antolín S. Paparrigópulos, so well known in the world of erudition.

I am not at all certain what kind of a reception Don Miguel's reading public will give to this novel or how they will take Don Miguel. For some time past I have been following the dispute which Don Miguel started with the innocent public, and I am truly astonished to discover how profoundly ingenuous this public is. Upon the publication of his articles in El Mundo Gráfico, *and of some similar articles, Don Miguel received letters and clippings from provincial papers which show clearly what treasures of ingenuous candor and of dovelike simplicity are still preserved among our people. In one of them there is a comment upon that remark of his to the effect that Señor Cervantes (Don Miguel) is not altogether lacking in genius, and the writer is scandalized by his irreverence. In another the writer is deeply moved by those melancholy reflections of his upon the fall of the leaves. Another is enthusiastic over his cry of "down with war," which was wrung from him by the pain of seeing men die without being killed. Others reproduce that bundle of quite unparadoxical truths which he printed after gathering them in the cafés and the clubs, where they had got rotten from mere handling and stank with the vulgarity of the atmosphere — because they recognize them as their own. And there was one guileless dove who was indignant because this logomachist, Don Miguel, sometimes writes Kulture with a capital K and, after claiming for himself a certain skill in the art of saying clever things, admits that he is unable to make up puns. Puns! Such is genius and artistic expression as conceived by the ingenuous public!*

It is just as well that the ingenuous public has taken no account, as it seems, of another of the deviltries of Don Miguel, who now and then likes to pose as clever. For example, he writes an article and then underscores some of the words at random, any words whatever, turning the pages upside-down so as not to know which words he is underscoring. When he told me of this I asked him why he had done it, and he said, "Oh, I don't know — for the fun of it — to turn a pirouette. And — besides, because words underscored and italicized annoy me and put me in a bad humour. That kind of thing amounts to insulting your reader and calling him dull. It is the same as saying, 'Brace up, man, and pay attention! This means something!' And this is why I advised a certain señor to print his articles all in italics so that the public might note that he meant every word most seriously, from first to last. This is simply pantomime in writing, an attempt to substitute gesture for accent and intonation. Look at the periodicals of the extreme right, friend Victor, those that are regarded as eminently sound, and you will see what an abuse they make of italics, small capitals, and capitals, of exclamation-points, and of all the various typographical resources. Pantomime! Pantomime! Pantomime! Such is the simplicity of their means of expression; or rather such is their sense of the ingenuous simplicity of their readers! It is time to have done with this ingenuousness!"

At other times I have heard Don Miguel maintain that what we call humour, or legitimate humour, has hardly taken root in Spain, nor will it easily do so in a long time to come. Those who are known here as humourists, he says, are sometimes satirists, at other times ironists — when they are not mere jokers. To call Taboada a humourist, for example, is to misuse the word. And there is nothing less humourous than the harsh, but clear and transparent, satire of Quevedo, in which the moral lesson is always immediately evident. Among those who could be called humourists we have had only one, namely, Cervantes, and if he came to life again how could he help laughing — said Don Miguel to *me — at those who were indignant because I found some genius in him? And above all how he must laugh at the ingenuous who have taken seriously some of his most subtle banter! For it is clear enough that it was part of his ridicule of the books of chivalry — very serious ridicule — to parody their style; and that passage, "Hardly had the rubicund Phoebus, etc.," which some ingenuous Cervantists offer as a model of style, is nothing more than a genial caricature of literary baroquism. I need hardly speak of the fashion of treating as an idiom such a passage as, "It was that of the dawn," with which he begins a chapter when the last chapter has ended with the word "hour."*

Our public, like every public of little education, is naturally suspicious, just as our people is suspicious. With us everybody is on his guard against letting another make a butt of him, or play him for a sucker, or put something over on him; and so, when a man begins to talk, we wish to know at once what to look for, and to know whether he is in jest or in earnest. I doubt if any other public is as much irritated by those who mix jest with earnest. Among ourselves who can stand it? It is very difficult for the average suspicious Spaniard to understand that a thing may be said in jest and in earnest at the same time, as a joke and at the same time seriously, and both from the same point of view.

Don Miguel is much interested in the idea of the comic-tragic, and he has told me more than once that he would not like to die without having written a tragic farce, or a farcical tragedy — not of the kind in which the farcical, or the grotesque, and the tragic are merely mixed and juxtaposed, but in which they are absolutely fused — and confused — into one. And when I called his attention to the fact that this was the most unbridled romanticism, he replied:

"I don't deny it; but you don't get anywhere by calling things names. In spite of twenty years spent in teaching the classics, the idea of a classicism which is opposed to a romanticism has never entered my head. They say that it is the part of the Greeks to distinguish, to define, to separate; it is my part, then, to indefine and confound."

And the basis of all this is simply a conception, or, better than a conception, an impression of life, which I dare not call pessimistic because I know that Don Miguel dislikes the word. It is his fixed *idea — and he is a monomaniac on the subject — that if his soul is not immortal, and if the souls of all other men, and even of all created things, are not immortal, and immortal in the very sense in which they were believed to be so by simple-minded Catholics in the Middle Ages, then — if this be not true — nothing has any value and nothing is worth the trouble. And from this came Leopardi's doctrine of tedium, after his last illusion had perished, namely,*

ch'io eterno mi credea,

the illusion of thinking himself eternal. And this explains why three of Don Miguel's favorite authors are Senancour, Quental, and Leopardi.

But this harsh and gloomy confusionist humourism, besides offending the sensibilities of those of our people who wish to know from the first word what to expect, is irritating to many other persons. People like to laugh, but mainly for the purpose of aiding digestion and of forgetting their troubles; not for the purpose of regurgitating what they ought not to have swallowed or of making it indigestible; still less for the purpose of digesting their troubles. And Don Miguel makes a point of this: that if you must make people laugh it should be not so that they may promote their digestion by contractions of the diaphragm, but that they may vomit what they have devoured; since one gets a clearer impression of life and of the world when the stomach is cleared of sweetmeats and of an excess of food. And he has no use for the irony that is without bitterness or for the humour that is discreet; for it is his opinion that where there is no bitterness there is no irony, and that discretionism necessarily quarrels with humourism, or, as he likes to call it, ill-humourism.

All of this involves taking upon himself a very disagreeable and rather thankless task, which he describes as a kind of massage of the ingenuous public with a view to discovering whether the collective intelligence of our people will not gradually become more agile and subtle. It irritates him beyond measure when it is said that our people is clever and ingenious, especially when this is said of the southerners. "A people that goes to bull-fights for its recreation and finds pleasure and variety in this primitive spectacle — from the standpoint of mentality this people is already judged."

And he goes on to say that it would be difficult to find a sillier or thicker mentality than that of the bull-fight enthusiast. Think of addressing a few paradoxical remarks, more or less humorous, to one who has just been delighted by a thrust of Vicente Pastor! And he loathes the lightsome manner of those who write the reviews of the bull-fights, high priests of the game of words and of all forms of refuse kitchen-wit.

If we add to this his delight in playing tricks with metaphysical concepts, we shall understand why there are so many people who turn from him in displeasure and refuse to read him; some persons because things of that kind give them a headache, others because, having in mind the saying that sacred subjects should be treated sacredly, sancta sancte tratanda sunt, *they think that these concepts ought not to furnish material for jesting and trifling. To this his reply is that he fails to understand why this insistence upon treating certain things seriously should come from the spiritual descendants of those who made a jest of the things that are most sacred, that is to say, of the most consoling beliefs and hopes of their fellows. If there*

*have been men who made a jest of God, why may
we not just as well make a jest of Reason, of Science, or even of Truth? If they have taken away
the dearest and innermost hope of our lives why
should we not go on to make confusion of everything, so as to kill time and eternity and get our
vengeance?*

*It may easily happen that someone will turn
up to say that this book contains passages that are
coarse, or, if you please, obscene. But Don Miguel
has taken care to have me say something about this
in the course of this nivola. And he is prepared to
protest against this imputation and to maintain
that any crudities that may be found here are for
the purpose, not of stimulating the appetites of our
sinful flesh, but only of furnishing a suggestion and
a point of departure for other considerations.*

*His repugnance to every form of obscenity is
well known to all who know him. And this not because of considerations conventionally moral, but
because he thinks that an erotic preoccupation is
that which of all things is most vitiating to the intelligence. The pornographic writers, or the simply
erotic, seem to him the least intelligent, the poorest*

in originality, in fact the silliest. I have heard him say that of the three vices of the classical triad, wine, women, and cards, the last two do more to weaken the mind than the first. And it is well known that Don Miguel drinks nothing but water. "One can talk to a drunken man," he once said to me. "He almost says something. But who can stand the conversation of a gambler or of one who runs after women? There is nothing lower except the conversation of the bull-fight enthusiast, which is the crown and peak of stupidity."

I am not surprised, however, by his suggesting a partnership between the erotic and the metaphysical, since I seem to know that our peoples began, as their literatures show, by being made up of warriors and saints, to be made up later of erotics and metaphysicians. The cult of woman coincided with the cult of conceptual subtleties. In the spiritual dawn of our peoples, that is to say, in the Middle Ages, the barbarian society had a sense of religious exaltation which was also mystical and warlike — the sword carried a cross in the hilt; but woman occupied a very small and very secondary place in its imagination, and the strictly philosophical ideas slumbered, enveloped in theology, off in the cloisters of convents and monasteries. The erotic and the metaphysical developed together. Religion is warlike in spirit; metaphysics is erotic or voluptuous.

It is the religious instinct that makes man bellicose and combative, or it may well be combativeness that makes him religious; and on the other hand it is the metaphysical instinct, a curious desire to know what does not concern us — the original sin, in short — that makes him sensual, though it may also be sensuality that awakens in him, as in Eve, the metaphysical instinct, a longing to possess the knowledge of good and evil. And then we have mysticism, a metaphysics of religion which is born of sensuality and combativeness.

This was well understood by the Athenian courtesan, Theodota, whose conversation with Socrates is related by Xenophon in his Memorabilia. *To Socrates, who was delighted with her method of investigation, or rather of assisting in the birth of truth, she proposed that he should become her* celestino *and help her in running down "friends."* (Synthérates, *fellow-hunter, the text reads, according to Don Miguel, professor of Greek, to whom I am indebted for this very interesting and en-*

lightening note.) And throughout this very interesting conversation between Theodota, the courtesan, and Socrates, the obstetrician-philosopher, one sees very clearly the intimate relationship that exists between the two professions, and how philosophy is in good large part pandering and pandering is also philosophy.

And if none of this is quite as I say, no one will deny that it is at least ingenious, and that is enough.

On the other hand I am not unaware that this distinction of mine between religion and bellicosity, on the one side, and philosophy and eroticism on the other, will be rejected by my dear master Don Fulgencio Entrambosmares del Aquilón, of whom Don Miguel has given such a detailed account in his novel, or nivola, Amor y Pedagogía. I presume that the illustrious author of the Arsmagna Combinatoria will establish the following possibilities: a bellicose religion and an erotic religion, a bellicose metaphysics and an erotic, a religious eroticism and a metaphysical eroticism, and a metaphysical bellicosism and a religious; and on the other hand a metaphysical religion and a religious metaphysics, a bellicose eroticism and an erotic bellicosism; all of this in addition to the religious religion, the metaphysical metaphysics, the erotic eroticism, and the bellicose bellicosism. The whole thing comes to sixteen binary combinations. We may omit the combinations of three, such as, for example, a metaphysico-erotic religion or a bellico-religious metaphysics. But I possess neither the inexhaustible genius for combinations of Don Fulgencio, nor, much less, the confusionist and indefinitionist impetuosity of Don Miguel.

There is much that I should like to say regarding the very unexpected ending of this tale and the version given there by Don Miguel of the death of my unfortunate friend Augusto, a version which I consider erroneous. But it is not a matter that I can undertake to discuss here in this prologue with the subject of my prologue. Yet to satisfy my conscience I must make it clear that I hold this conviction: namely, that Augusto Pérez, in fulfilment of the intention of committing suicide, which he communicated to me in the last interview that I had with him, did really commit suicide, as a matter of fact, and not merely in idea, by virtue of his desire to do so. I think that I have convincing proofs in support of my opinion; so many proofs indeed, and of such a character, that it ceases to be a matter of opinion and becomes a matter of knowledge.

With this I conclude.

VICTOR GOTI.

POST-PROLOGUE

I should very much like to discuss here some of the statements of my prologist, Victor Goti, but since I am in the secret of his existence I prefer to leave to him the entire responsibility for what he says in the prologue. Since, moreover, it was I who asked him to write it, thus committing myself beforehand (or, say, a priori) *to accepting just what he would write, there is no way in which I can reject it now after the fact (or, say, a* posteriori), *or perhaps even revise it. But that I should let certain opinions of his pass without adding my own, is another matter.*

I hardly know how far it is proper to make use of confidences communicated under the bond of intimate friendship and to give to the public, opinions and ideas which were not expressed with a view to publication. But Goti has committed the indiscretion of making known in his prologue certain judgments of mine which I never intended to become public. Or at least I never wished him to publish them in the crude state in which I expounded them privately.

Regarding his statement that the unfortu-

nate — *Yet why unfortunate? Well, granting that he was unfortunate, the statement, I say, that Augusto Pérez, unfortunate or whatever he was, committed suicide, and did not die in the manner in which I relate the story of his death, that is to say, absolutely as the result of my own decision and of my own free will* — *this statement makes me smile. There are some opinions, of course, which deserve only a smile. But it would be well for my friend and prologist Goti to be careful about questioning my decisions. For if he annoys me very much I shall end by doing to him what I did to his friend Pérez: I shall either let him die or kill him* — *after the fashion of the doctors. For, as my readers know, the doctors face this dilemma: either they must let their patient die for fear that they may kill him, or they must kill him so that he may not die on their hands. And thus I too am capable of killing Goti if I see that he is going to die on my hands, or of letting him die if I fear that I may have to kill him.*

Having said enough to explain this dilemma to my friend Victor Goti — *whom I wish to thank for his trouble* — *I have no wish to carry this post-prologue further.* M . DE U .

I

A U G U S T O appeared at the door of his house and held out his right hand with the palm downward. Turning his eyes towards the sky he remained for a moment fixed in that august and statuesque attitude. This did not signify that he was taking possession of the external world; he was merely looking to see if it was raining. And as he felt on the back of his hand the freshness of a slight drizzle his brow contracted. It was not because he was discommoded by the mere drizzle, but because he had to open his umbrella. Folded snugly within its cover, the umbrella seemed so slender and elegant. An umbrella closed is as elegant as an open umbrella is ugly.

"It is a misfortune," thought Augusto, "that we need the services of things and have to make use of them. All beauty is marred by use, if not destroyed. The noblest function of things is that of being contemplated. How beautiful is an orange before dinner! In heaven all this will be changed. There our function will be reduced, rather it will be broadened into that of contemplating God and all things in him. Here, in this wretched life, we think only of putting God to use; we try to open him as we do an umbrella, in order that he may protect us from all sorts of evils."

Having thus spoken he stooped to turn up his trousers. Finally he opened his umbrella and remained for a moment uncertain, wondering within himself, "And now in which direction shall I go? To the right or to the left?" For Augusto was less of a traveller through life than a saunterer. "I will wait until a dog passes," he said, "and I will start out in the direction that he takes."

Just then there passed down the street, not a dog, but a handsome young woman, and following the attraction of her eyes went Augusto, as if drawn by a magnet, without knowing what he was doing.

And so down one street, and another, and another.

"That urchin," Augusto went along saying to himself — talking to himself rather than thinking, "what is he doing there with his face down close to the ground? Looking at the ants, of course! The ant, bah! The most hypocritical of all animals. All that he does is to walk about and make us believe that he is working. Like this loafer coming along here, walking as if he were in a hurry and elbowing all the people that he meets: I am quite sure that he has nothing at all to do. What can he have to do, what could he have to do anyhow? He

is an idler, an idler like — No, I am not an idler.
My imagination never takes a rest. The idlers are
those who pretend to work and then do nothing
but daze themselves and stifle thought. For look
now, this freak of a chocolate man, who sets himself, here behind this show-window, where all may
see him, to turn this stupid cylinder — this exhi-
bitionist of work, what is he but an idler? And
what difference does it make to us whether he works
or not? Work! Work! Hypocrisy! As far as work
goes, the work done by this poor paralytic, half
dragging himself along here —— But what am I
thinking about? Forgive me, brother" — this he
said aloud — "Brother? Brother in what? In paraly-
sis? They say we are all sons of Adam. And this Joa-
quinito, is he also a son of Adam? Good-bye, Joa-
quin. There now, the inevitable automobile with its
noise and dust! What do they get out of shortening
distance in this fashion? The mania for travelling
comes not from philotopia, but from topophobia.
He who gives himself up to travel is never seeking
the place that he is going to, but only fleeing from
the place that he has left. Travel! Travel! What
a nuisance is an umbrella! But stop, what is
this?"

He found himself before the door of a house
which had just been entered by the handsome
young woman who was pulling him along magne-
tized by the attraction of her eyes. And then for

the first time Augusto discovered that he had been following her. The *concierge* of the house looked at him out of her small, cunning eyes, and that look suggested to Augusto what he ought to do. "This female Cerberus," he said to himself, "is waiting for me to ask her the name of the señorita that I have been pursuing, and all about her; and certainly this is what it is now up to me to do. Anything else would leave the pursuit unrewarded, and I can't do that; things have to be finished. I hate all incompleteness." He put his hand into his pocket and found nothing less than a *duro*. It was hardly feasible just then to go elsewhere and have it changed; he would lose time and miss his opportunity.

"Tell me, good woman," he inquired of the *concierge*, without taking his thumb and forefinger out of his pocket, "could you give me, in confidence and *inter nos*, the name of the señorita who has just gone in?"

"There is no secret about that, sir, and there would be nothing wrong in telling you."

"Then tell me."

"Well, her name is Doña Eugenia Domingo del Arco."

"Domingo? It must be Dominga."

"No, señor, Domingo; her first surname is Domingo."

"But in the case of a woman the surname

ought to be changed to Dominga. Otherwise what becomes of the agreement in gender?"

"I don't know anything about that, señor."

"And tell me — tell me" — without taking his fingers from his pocket, "how is it that she goes out alone? Is she married or single? Has she parents?"

"She is single, and she is an orphan. She lives with an aunt and uncle."

"On the father's side or on the mother's?"

"All that I know is that they are an aunt and uncle."

"That is enough."

"She gives piano-lessons for a living."

"And does she play well?"

"That is more than I know."

"Good, very good, that will do. And take this for your trouble."

"Thank you, señor, thank you. Is there anything more that I can do for you? Is there any way in which I can be of use to you? Do you wish me to take a message?"

"Perhaps — perhaps — but not now. Goodday."

"You may make use of me, sir, and count upon my absolute discretion."

"Well, sir!" said Augusto to himself as he left the *concierge*, "see how I have got myself tied up with this good woman. For as a matter of dignity

I can't drop the matter here. If I do, what will this pattern of a *concierge* say of me? And so — Eugenia Dominga — I mean Domingo — del Arco? Very well, I shall make a note of it so as not to forget it. The art of mnemonics consists in carrying a note-book in your pocket. That was what my ever-memorable Don Leoncio used to say: never put into your head what you can carry in your pocket. To which one might add the complementary proposition: never put into your pocket what you can carry in your head. But now this *concierge* — what's the name of the *concierge?*"

He retraced his steps.

"Tell me one thing more, my good woman."

"At your service."

"Your own name — what is your name?"

"Mine? Margarita."

"Very good, very good—thank you."

"Don't mention it."

Augusto resumed his walk and found himself after a little time in the Paseo de la Alameda.

The slight rain has ceased. He closed his umbrella, folded it up, and put it into the cover. He approached a bench, and touching it he found it to be damp. He took a newspaper from his pocket, spread it out over the bench and sat down. Then he took out his note-book, and flourishing his fountain-pen before his face, he said, "Here's a most useful toy." Without it I should have to put down the name of this señorita in pencil, and then it might be rubbed out. Will her image ever be erased from my memory? But what is she like? This sweet Eugenia, what does she look like? All that I seem to remember is a pair of eyes. I seem to feel the contact of those eyes — While I was indulging in lyrical divagations there were eyes tugging gently at my heart. Let me see, Eugenia Domingo — yes, Domingo — del Arco. Domingo? I can't get used to the idea that her name is Domingo — No, I shall have to get her to change her name and call herself Dominga. But what about our sons? Will they have to bear the name of Dominga as their second surname? And since they will wish to get rid of this name of mine, this absurd Pérez, leaving only a P., will our first-born be named Augusto P. Dominga? But — this crazy brain of mine, where is it taking me?" And he entered in his note-book, "Eugenia Domingo del Arco, Avenida de la Alameda, 58." Just above this entry stood these two hendecasyllabic lines:

"From the cradle comes our sadness and our sorrow
And from the cradle too our joy and gladness. . . ."

"Here now!" said Augusto to himself, "this Eugenita, the piano-teacher, has cut short an excellent beginning that I had made of some transcendental lyric poetry. My poetry is interrupted. Interrupted? — Yes, all that men can do is to seek in the course of events, in the vicissitudes of their lot, nutriment for the sadness or joy with which they were born; and whether a thing is sad or joyful depends upon inborn disposition. And now about Eugenia? I must write to her. But not from this place; no, from my home. Or had I better go to the Casino? No, I'll go home — home. Things of this kind should come from the home, from the hearth. From the hearth? My house is not a hearth. Hearth? — hearth? It is more like an ash-bin. Ah, my Eugenia!"

And Augusto returned home.

II

*W*H E N the man-servant opened the door——

Augusto, who was rich and alone in the world, his mother having died not more than six months before the occurrence of these insignificant events, lived with a man-servant and a cook, old dependants of the house and children of former retainers in the same family. The man-servant and the cook were man and wife, but childless.

When the servant opened the door Augusto asked him if anyone had called in his absence.

"No one, señorito,"

This question and answer were part of a ritual; for hardly anyone called upon Augusto in his home.

He went to his sitting-room, took an envelope, and wrote upon it: "Señorita Doña Eugenia Domingo del Arco. To be delivered into her own hands." And then with the blank paper before him he rested his head upon both hands, his elbows on the desk, and closed his eyes. "Let me first call up her picture," he said. And he made an effort to catch in the darkness the splendour of those other eyes that had caught him up and carried him along at random.

He remained for some time in this position trying to recall the face of Eugenia; and since he had hardly seen her face he had to reconstruct it in imagination. Thanks to this process of evocation, there arose gradually before him the rather errant image of a face encircled by dreams. And then he fell asleep. He fell asleep because he had passed a bad night, a night troubled by insomnia.

"Señorito!"

"Eh?" cried Augusto awaking.

"Lunch is already served."

Was it the servant's voice that woke him, or was it his appetite, of which the voice was merely an echo? "Psychological mysteries!" So thought Augusto, who went into the dining-room saying to himself, "Ah, this psychology!"

He ate with a relish his everyday lunch, a couple of fried eggs, a beefsteak with potatoes, and a bit of Gruyère cheese. Then he took his coffee and stretched himself out in a rocking-chair. He lighted a cigar, put it into his mouth, and saying to himself, "Ah, my Eugenia!" he gave himself to thinking about her.

"My Eugenia. Yes, mine," he continued saying to himself. "This one that I am forging for myself, and not that other one, not the one of flesh and bone, not the one that I saw pass the door of

my house, a chance apparition, not the *concierge's*
Eugenia. A chance apparition? But what apparition may that not be? And what is the logic of ap-
paritions? It is the same as the logic of this succession of figures formed by the smoke of my cigar.
Chance! Chance is the inner rhythm of the world;
chance is the soul of poetry. Ah, my chanceful
Eugenia! This life of mine, quiet, modest, and rou-
tine, is a Pindaric ode woven of the thousand trifles
of daily events. Daily events! Give us this day our
daily bread! Give me, O Lord, the thousand small
events of each day. It is not the great pains, nor
the great joys, to which we succumb; and this is
because the great pains and the great joys come
wrapped in a vast mist of trifling incidents. And
life is just this — mist. Life is a nebula. And out of
it now arises Eugenia. But who is Eugenia? Ah, it
begins to dawn upon me that for some time past
I have been looking for her. And while I was in the
process of looking for her, there she turned up right
in front of me. Isn't that what you mean by finding something? When one discovers an apparition
that one was looking for, is it not because the apparition, in sympathy with the search, comes out to
meet one? Did not America come out to look for
Columbus? And hasn't Eugenia come to look for
me? Eugenia, Eugenia, Eugenia!"

And Augusto caught himself uttering the
name of Eugenia aloud. Upon hearing him speak,

the man-servant, who happened to be passing near the dining-room, came in and asked:

"Was the señorito calling?"

"No, I wasn't calling you. But wait a moment, don't you call yourself Domingo?"

"Yes, señorito," replied Domingo, not at all surprised by the question put to him.

"And why do you call yourself Domingo?"

"Because that is what they call me."

"Good, very good," said Augusto to himself. "We call ourselves by what they call us. In the days of Homer both persons and things had two names, one that men gave them and the other given by the gods. I wonder what God can be calling me. And why am I not to call myself differently from what others call me? Why should I not give Eugenia a name different from what others name her, different from the name given by Margarita, the *concierge*? And what shall I call her?"

"You may go," he said to the servant.

He rose from the rocking-chair, went into his sitting-room, took a pen and sat down to write:

"Señorita: This very morning, beneath the gentle rain from heaven, you, a chance apparition, passed in front of the door of the house where I live indeed but have no home. When I awoke it was at the door of your house, in which I do not know whether you have a home or not. Your eyes had carried me there; your eyes, twin refulgent stars in the nebula of my world. Forgive me, Eugenia, and permit me to address you familiarly by this sweet name; forgive my lyrical tone. I live in a perpetual infinitessimal lyricism.

"I do not know what more to say to you. But, yes, I do know. But I have so much, so very much to say to you that I think it better to postpone it until we can meet and talk together. For that is what I now desire, that we may see one another, talk with one another, write to one another, and learn to know one another. And then — then God and our own hearts will tell us.

"Will you hear me then, Eugenia, sweet apparition of my daily life, will you hear me?

"Shrouded in the mist of my life, I await your reply.

Augusto Pérez."

As he signed his name he said to himself, "This fashion of signing your name with a flourish pleases me because it is so useless."

He sealed the letter and went out again into the street.

"Thanks be to God," he said to himself as he passed down the Avenida de la Alameda, "thanks be to God that I know now where I am going and that I have somewhere to go. This Eugenia of mine is a blessing from God. She has now brought a purpose and a goal into my wandering about the streets. Now I have a house to haunt and a *concierge* who is my confidential agent."

While he was thus talking to himself he passed Eugenia without noticing even the splendour of her eyes. The mist in his soul was altogether too dense. Eugenia, however, took note of him and said to herself, "Who can this young fellow be? His manner and bearing are not bad, and he seems to be well-to-do." And it happened that, without clearly knowing why, she guessed that he was someone who had followed her that morning. Women always know when you are looking at them, even when you fail to see them; and they know too when you see them without looking at them.

And the two of them, Augusto and Eugenia, passed on in opposite directions, cutting through with their souls the tangled spiritual web of the street. For the street forms a web in which are cross-woven looks of desire, of envy, of disdain, of compassion, of love, of hate; words of ancient import whose meaning has become crystallized; thoughts and aspirations; all forming a mysterious fabric enshrouding the souls of those who pass along.

Finally Augusto found himself once more in the presence of the *concierge,* Margarita, and in the presence of Margarita's smile. The first thing that

she did when she saw him was to take her hand
out of the pocket of her apron.

"Good evening, Margarita."

"Good evening, señorito."

"Augusto, my good woman, Augusto."

"Don Augusto," she added.

"The 'Don' doesn't fit every name," he ob-
served. "There's a great gulf between Juan and Don
Juan, and just as great a gulf between Augusto and
Don Augusto. But — let it pass. Has the Señorita
Eugenia gone out?"

"Yes, a moment ago."

"In what direction?"

"In this direction."

And in this direction went Augusto likewise.
But after a moment he returned. He had forgotten
the letter.

"Do me the favor, Señora Margarita, to see
that this letter is put into Señorita Eugenia's own
fair hands."

"With great pleasure."

"But into her own fair hands, you understand?
Into those hands as like unto ivory as the piano-
keys which they caress."

"Yes, I understand. I have had the same thing
to do before."

"Before? What do you mean by doing it before?"

"But does the gentleman think that this is the first letter of this kind? —— "

"Of this kind? But do you know what kind of a letter mine is?"

"Of course. I knew it at once — just like the others."

"The others? What do you mean by the others?"

"But you don't suppose that you are the first admirer the señorita has had!"

"Ah! But she is free now?"

"Now? No, no, señor, now she has a fiancé or something of the sort — although I think he is only an admirer who hopes to become her fiancé. . . . But perhaps she is only trying him out — it may be that he is only for a time —— "

"And why did you not tell me?"

"Because you didn't ask me."

"True, I didn't. Nevertheless deliver this letter, and into her own hands, you understand? We'll fight for her! And there is another *duro.*"

"Thank you, señor, thank you."

It cost Augusto some effort to tear himself away, for the nebulous, everyday conversation of Margarita, the *concierge,* was beginning to be pleasant to him. Was this not one way of killing time?"

"We'll fight for her!" Augusto went on saying to himself on his way down the street. "Yes, we'll fight for her! And so she has another fiancé,

or lover, or at least an aspirant for her hand. We'll
fight for her! *Militia est vita hominum super ter-
ram,* the life of man on earth is a life of warfare.
Now my life has a purpose; now I have a conquest
to make and carry to the end. Oh, Eugenia, my
Eugenia, you are to be mine! At least, *my* Eugenia,
this Eugenia that I have forged out of the passing
vision of those eyes, out of that conjunction of stars
in my nebula — this Eugenia is certainly to be mine,
whoever may get the other Eugenia, the Eugenia of
the *concierge.* We'll fight! We'll fight, and I shall
win, for I know the secret of victory. Ah, Eugenia,
my Eugenia!"

And he found himself at the door of the Casino, where Victor was already waiting for him to
play their daily game of chess.

III

Y O U are a little late today, my boy," said Victor to Augusto. "You who are always so punctual."

"Why, yes, to be sure — business —— "

"Business! You?"

"Do you think that nobody but stock-brokers has business to attend to? Life is much more complex than you imagine."

"Or simpler than you perhaps think —— "

"It might be anything."

"Very well, play!"

Augusto moved the king's pawn two squares forward; and instead of humming bits of the opera as he usually did, he kept saying to himself, "Eugenia, Eugenia, Eugenia, my Eugenia, the final purpose of my life, sweet splendour of twin stars in the mist, we'll fight for her! Certainly there is logic here, in this game of chess; and yet how nebulous it is after all, and how much a matter of chance! Perhaps there is an element of chance and of venture in logic itself. And that apparition of my Eugenia, may there not be something logical about that? May it not be a part of some divine game of chess?"

"But, old man!" interrupted Victor. "Isn't it agreed that you can't take a move back? A piece touched is a piece played."

"That's understood, of course."

"But if you make that move I get your bishop for nothing."

"True, true! I was a bit distracted."

"But you mustn't be distracted. Playing chess is not roasting chestnuts. But you know, of course, that a piece touched is a piece played."

"Yes, to be sure; it can't be helped now."

"And it ought to be so. That is what makes the game so educational."

"And why shouldn't one be distracted in playing a game?" said Augusto to himself. "Is life a game or is it not? And why can't we take a play back? That's where the logic comes in. Perhaps by this time Eugenia has received the letter. *Alea jacta est,* the die is cast! What's done is done! And to-morrow? Tomorrow is in the hands of God. But yesterday — to whom does that belong? Whose was yesterday? Ah, yesterday, the treasure of the strong! Blessed yesterday, substance and support of the mist of day-by-day!"

"Check!" interrupted Victor.

"True, true, let me see —— But how did I let things come to such a pass?"

"By being distracted, man, as usual. If you weren't so distracted you would be one of our best players."

"But tell me, Victor, is life a game or is it only a distraction?"

"But a game itself is only a distraction."

"Then what difference does it make whether you get your distraction in one way or another?"

"Man, if you play at all, you must play well."

"But why may not one play badly? And what does it mean to play well or to play badly? Why shouldn't we move these pieces in some other way than the way we do?"

"This is the theory of the game, friend Augusto, in accordance with which you, a noted philosopher, have taught me to play it."

"Very well, now I am going to give you a great piece of news."

"Out with it!"

"But be prepared to be surprised, my boy."

"I am not one of those who are surprised *a priori*, or before the fact."

"Well, here goes. Do you know what is happening to me?"

"I know that you are getting all the time more and more distracted."

"Well, it happens that I have fallen in love."

"Bah! I knew that already."

"How did you know it?"

"Quite simply. You have been in love *ab origine,* from the time you were born. You have an inborn love-sickness."

"Yes, love is born with us when we are born."

"I didn't say love, but love-sickness. And I already knew that you had fallen in love, or rather that you were infatuated, without your having to tell me. I knew it better than you did yourself."

"But with whom? Tell me, with whom?"

"You don't know any more about that than I do."

"Well, keep quiet and listen to me. You may be right —— "

"Didn't I tell you? And if not, tell me, is she blonde or brunette?"

"Well, the truth is, I don't know. Yet as I seem to see her, she's neither one nor the other. It's this way — her hair is a chestnut colour."

"Is she tall or short?"

"I don't remember that either. But I think she must be of medium height. But, my boy, what eyes! What eyes my Eugenia has!"

"Eugenia?"

"Yes, Eugenia Domingo del Arco, Avenida de la Alameda, 58."

"The piano-teacher?"

"The same. But —— "

"Yes, I know her. And now — check again!"

"But —— "

"Check, I say!"

"Very well, then."

Augusto covered the king with a knight and finished by losing the game.

As Victor took leave of Augusto he made a yoke of his right hand, and placing it over the nape of Augusto's neck, he whispered, "And so it is Eugenita, the piano-teacher, eh? Good for you, Augustito! you are to possess the earth."

"These diminutives — these terrible diminutives!" thought Augusto as he passed out into the street.

IV

"W H Y is the diminutive a mark of affection?" — Augusto was talking to himself on the way home. "Can it be that love makes the loved one childish? And so I have fallen in love! It has happened to me! Who would have said so? But can Victor be right in saying that I am in love *ab origine?* Well, it may be true that my love has preceded its object. What is more, it is perhaps this love of mine that has called up its object and brought it out of the mist of creation. But if I move that rook forward, he can't checkmate me, he can't possibly. And what is love? Who has ever defined love? Love once defined would cease to be love. But, heavens, why will the mayor permit them to put on their sign-boards letters as ugly as these? That bishop was played badly. And how can I have fallen in love with her if I really can't say that I know her? Bah! the knowledge will come later. Love comes before knowledge, and knowledge kills love. *Nihil volitum quin praecognitum,* as Padre Zaramillo used to say; nothing is willed which has not first been known. But I have reached the opposite conclusion, namely, that nothing is known which has not first been willed: *nihil cog-nitum quin praevolitum*. To understand is to forgive, they say. No, to forgive is to understand. First comes love and then understanding. But how was it that I did not see that he would give me mate by discovery? And if you are to love anything what is first necessary? To get a glimpse of it! A glimpse — behold, then, the intuition of love: a glimpse through the mist. Later come the clearer outlines, the perfect vision — that is to say, when you resolve the mist into drops of water, or into sleet or snow, or into hail. Science is a hail-storm. No, no, mist, mist! If one could only be an eagle so as to sweep through the bosom of the clouds! And see the sun through the clouds, as a luminary also nebulous.

"Oh, the eagle! The eagle of Patmos and the owl of Minerva — when the eagle of Patmos, which looks the sun in the face but sees nothing in the darkness of the night, had stolen away from the presence of St. John and met the owl of Minerva, which sees in the dark but cannot look at the sun, and had escaped from Olympus, think of what they must have said to one another!"

At this point in his reflections Augusto passed Eugenia in the street and failed to see her.

"Knowledge comes later," he continued to himself. "But — what was that? I could swear that a pair of mystically refulgent twin stars had crossed

my orbit. Could it have been she? My heart tells
me —— But stop, here I am at home."

He entered the house.

He went straight to his bedroom and threw
himself on the bed. "Alone!" he reflected. "Think
of sleeping alone, dreaming alone! When persons
sleep together it must be that they dream in common. Mysterious effluvia must unite the two brains.
Or may it not be perhaps that the more the hearts
are united, the more the heads are separated? Perhaps. They may be in inverse proportion. If two
lovers think alike their feelings will be the opposite of each other. If they partake of communion
in the same amorous sentiment, each of them will
be thinking something different and perhaps opposite. The woman loves her man just so far as he
does not think like her, that is to say, so far as he
thinks. Ah, but here's this worthy married couple!
I'll step in and see them.

In the evening before going to bed Augusto
often played a game of ombre with his servant,
Domingo, while the cook, his wife, looked on.

The game began.

"Twenty in hearts," droned Domingo.

"Tell me," Augusto exclaimed suddenly.
"What if I should marry?"

"It would be a very good thing, señorito," said
Domingo.

"It all depends," his wife, Liduvina, ventured to insinuate.

"But didn't you get married yourself?" replied Augusto.

"It all depends, señorito."

"Depends upon what? Tell me."

"It is very easy to get married, but it's not so easy after you are married."

"This belongs to that popular wisdom which is the fountain of —— "

"And the sort of person the señorito's wife should be —— " added Liduvina, fearing that Augusto was about to pour forth a monologue.

"What sort? What is the sort that my wife should be? Come, tell me!"

"Well, since the señorito is so good —— "

"Go on and tell me, woman, tell me at once."

"You remember, don't you, what the señora used to say —— "

At this reverent reminder of his mother Augusto dropped the cards upon the table and his thoughts remained for a moment suspended. Many times had that gentle lady, his mother, daughter of misfortune — many times had she said to him: "I cannot live much longer, my son; your father is calling me. Perhaps he has greater need of me than you. As soon as I have departed from the world and you are left alone in it, I wish you to marry, to marry as soon as possible. Bring to this house one who shall be mistress and lady of the house. And it is not that I do not trust our old and faithful servants — no, not for a moment. But there should be a mistress in the house. And she should be a house-keeper, my son, mistress of the house and house-keeper. Make her the keeper of your heart, of your purse, of your larder, and of your resolutions. Look for a managing woman, one who will know how to love you — and to manage you."

"My wife will play the piano," said Augusto, shaking himself free from the memories that were making him homesick.

"The piano! And what's the good of that?" asked Liduvina.

"What's the good of it? Why, that's just what constitutes its greatest charm, that there's not a damned bit of good in it. It is of no service, as they say. And I am sick of services —— "

"Of ours?"

"No, not of yours; by no means. And more-over the piano serves, yes, it serves — it serves to fill the fireside with harmony and keep it from being an ash-pit."

"Harmony! And how can you eat that?"

"Liduvina — Liduvina —— !"

The cook bowed her head before this gentle reproof. It was a way the two of them had with each other.

"Yes, she will play the piano because she is a piano-teacher."

"Then she won't play it," affirmed Liduvina positively. "Or why should she get married?"

"My Eugenia —— " began Augusto.

"Ah! And so her name is Eugenia, and she is a teacher of piano?" asked the cook.

"Yes, what of it?"

"The one who lives with an aunt and uncle in the Avenida de la Alameda, over the shop of Señor Tiburcio?"

"The same. What! do you know her."

"Yes — by sight —— "

"No, tell me something more, Liduvina, tell me more. Come, tell me. Remember that it is something that concerns your master's whole future happiness —— "

"She is a good girl, yes, a good girl —— "

"Come, tell me, Liduvina — for my mother's sake! —— "

"Remember what the señora counselled you, señorito —— But what's that running about in the kitchen? What is the cat up to? —— "

The servant rose and left the room.

"Well, shall we finish the game?" asked Domingo.

"That's so, Domingo. We can't leave it where it is. Whose turn is it to play?"

"Yours, señorito."

"Well, here goes."

And he lost this game too, out of sheer distraction.

"Well, sir!" he said to himself as he went to his bedroom. "Everybody knows her — everybody except me. Such is the way of love. And tomorrow? What shall I do tomorrow? Bah! Sufficient unto the day is the evil thereof. And now to bed."

And he got into bed.

After he was in bed he continued talking to himself: "It seems to be the case that I have been boring myself to death without knowing it — and for two mortal years past, ever since my sainted mother died. Yes, yes, there is such a thing as an unconscious tedium. Nearly all of us are boring ourselves unconsciously. Tedium is the foundation of life, and it is tedium that has invented all the games and distractions, the novels, and love. The mist of life precipitates a gentle tedium in the form of a bitter-sweet liquor. All these insignificant everyday events, all these mild conversations by which we kill time and prolong life, what are they but the gentlest way of boring ourselves? Oh, Eugenia, my Eugenia, flower of the unconscious tedium which is the substance of my life, be with me in my dreams, dream with me and within me!"

And he fell asleep.

v

*H*E swept through the clouds, a shining eagle, his powerful wings pearled with dew, his preying eyes fixed upon the solar mist, his heart asleep in a sweet tedium, protected by a breast steeled by the storms; round about him the silence created by the murmurs from the distant earth, and there above him, at the zenith of the heavens, two twin stars diffusing an invisible balm. The silence was rent by a strident cry of *"La Correspondencia!* —— " And Augusto glimpsed the light of a new day.

"Am I dreaming or am I alive?" he asked himself, wrapping the blanket around him. "Am I an eagle or am I a man? I wonder what there will be in that newspaper. What new things will the new day bring along to me? Will an earthquake have swallowed up Corcubion in the night? Then why not Leipzig? Ah, this lyric association, this Pindaric disorder of ideas! The world is a kaleidoscope. It is man that puts logic into it. The supreme art is the art of chance. Let me sleep a while longer, then." And he turned half over in bed.

"La Correspondencia —— " The vinegar man.

And then a carriage, and afterwards an automobile, and after that some small boys.

"Impossible!" said Augusto finally. "This is the return of life. And with it the return of love — And what is love? Isn't love perhaps the distillation of it all? Is it not the essence of the tedium? Let me think about Eugenia; the time is propitious for it."

And he closed his eyes with the intention of thinking about Eugenia. Of thinking?

But this thinking of his underwent a process of dilution and dissolution, and very soon it was nothing more than a polka. The fact was that a street-piano had halted under the window of his bedroom and was giving forth sounds. And the soul of Augusto was beating time to notes; he was not thinking.

"The essence of the world is musical," Augusto said to himself when the last note of the piano had died away. "And my Eugenia, isn't she musical too? Every law is a law of rhythm, and rhythm is love. Behold, then, how the divine morning, the virginity of the day, brings me a discovery: love is rhythm! The science of rhythm is mathematics: the sensuous expression of love is music. The expression, of course, not the realization."

A tap at the door interrupted him.

"Come in!"

"Did you call, señorito?" said Domingo.

"Yes — my breakfast!"

He had called, without noting the fact, at least an hour and a half earlier than usual, and having once called he had to ask for his breakfast, although it was not time for it.

"Love stimulates and quickens the appetite," Augusto went on saying to himself. "One must live in order to love. Yes, and one must love in order to live."

He got up to take his breakfast.

"What's the weather like, Domingo?"

"Just the same as usual."

"Ah, yes! neither good nor bad."

"Just so."

This was the adopted theory of the servant — who also had theories.

Augusto washed, dressed, brushed his hair, and groomed himself generally like a man who had now an objective in the world and was overflowing with an inner relish for life. Yet a somewhat melancholy relish.

He went into the street, and soon his heart was beating violently. "Let me think!" he said to himself. "Surely I had seen her before, I knew her for a long time; yes, her image is almost inborn in me! — Mother, help me!" And when Eugenia passed close to him as he met her on the street he saluted her rather more with his eyes than with his hat.

He was about to turn back and follow her,

but his better judgment prevailed, and also his desire for a little gossip with the *concierge*.

"It is she, yes, it's she," he continued saying to himself. "She's the very one — the one that I was looking for long ago, though I never knew it. And she is the one that was looking for me. We were destined for each other, in a pre-established harmony; we are two monads complementary to one another. The family is the true social cell — and I am nothing but a molecule. Goodness, how much poetry there is in science! Oh, Mother, Mother, behold here your son; give him your counsel from heaven! Eugenia, my Eugenia! —— "

He looked all about him to see if anyone were looking, and then he surprised himself by embracing the air. And he said to himself: "Love is an ecstasy; it takes us out of ourselves."

He was brought back to reality — to reality? — by the smile of Margarita.

"Well, is there no news?" Augusto asked her.

"None, señorito, it is still rather early."

"Didn't she ask any questions when you gave it to her?"

"None."

"And today?"

"Yes, today she did. She asked me for your address, and whether I knew you, and who you were. She said that the señorito had not remembered to put down the street and number of his house. And then she gave me a message —— "

"A message? What was it? Don't hesitate."

"She told me that if you came again I should say that she is already engaged and has a fiancé."

"That she has a fiancé?"

"I told you so before, señorito."

"Never mind. We'll fight for her!"

"Very well, we'll fight for her."

"Do you promise to help me, Margarita?"

"Of course I do."

"Then we shall win."

He left her and went to the Alameda to quiet his emotions in the greenness of the shrubbery and in hearing the birds sing their loves. His heart was young and fresh, and within him were singing too, like the nightingales, the winged memories of his infancy.

Above all else stood the heaven of his recollections of his mother, shedding a sweetly dissolving light upon all his other memories.

His father he hardly remembered; a mythic shade losing itself in the far distance; a blood-stained sunset cloud. Blood-stained, because while still a very small boy he remembered seeing him bathed in blood, from a hæmorrhage, with the face of a corpse. And his heart still resounded, from so long ago, with that "My son!" of his mother which rent the house; that "My son!" which left him un-

certain whether it was addressed to his dying father
or to himself, to Augusto petrified by incompre-
hension before the mystery of death.

A little later his mother, trembling with grief,
pressed him to her bosom, and with a litany of "My
son! My son! My son!" baptized him in tears of
fire. And he wept also, clinging close to his mother,
and not daring to turn his head or to take it out of
the sweet darkness of that palpitating breast, for
fear of encountering the devouring eyes of the
Coco.

And so passed days of weeping and of darkness, until the tears began retreating within and the
house began to dissipate the gloom.

It was a sweetly restful house. The light found
its way in between the white flowers embroidered
upon the curtains. The chairs opened their arms
with the familiarity of grandsires made children by
the passage of the years. Here lay an ash-tray still
with the ashes of the last cigar his father had consumed. And there, on the wall, a portrait of both,
of the father and of the mother, now a widow,
taken on the very day of their wedding. He, who
was tall, was seated, with one leg crossed over the
other, showing the tongue of his boot, and she,
who was short, was standing by his side and resting a finely shaped hand — a hand made, not for
grasping, but only for perching, like the foot of a
dove — upon the shoulder of her husband.

His mother always moved about noiselessly, like a bird; dressed always in black, with a smile, the sediment of the tears of those early days of widowhood, on her lips and round about her longing, questing eyes. "I have to live for you, Augusto, for you alone," she used to say to him in the evening before going to bed. And he carried into his dreams of the night a kiss still moist with tears.

Life passed along for them like a gentle dream.

In the evening his mother used to read to him, sometimes the life of a saint, at other times a novel of Jules Verne, or some tale simple and sincere. And sometimes she almost laughed, with a silent and gentle laugh that rose above the tears in the distance.

In time he entered the Instituto, and in the evenings it was his mother who heard his lessons. And she studied them so as to be able to hear them with him. She studied all those strange names in general history, and she used to say to him, smiling, "But, Lord, what a host of barbarities men have been capable of committing!" She studied mathematics, and it was there that the gentle mother excelled. "If my mother should make a specialty of mathematics —— " Augusto used to say to himself. And he remembered the interest with which she used to follow the development of an equation of the second degree. She studied psychology, and this was what she found least intelligible. "But what a passion for making things complicated!" she used to say about this. She studied physics and chemistry and natural science. What she did not like about natural science was the strange names they gave to the animals and the plants. Physiology horrified her, and she gave up hearing her son's lessons in that subject. Merely looking at the plates showing the heart or the lungs uncovered brought back to her the bloody death of her husband. "All this is very repulsive, my son," she said to him. "Don't study medicine. It is better not to know what things are like inside."

When Augusto graduated from the Instituto she took him in her arms, gazed at the down upon his lip, and said, "if only your father were living! —— " Afterwards she made him sit upon her knee, of which he, now a big boy, was rather ashamed, and she held him thus, in silence, with her eyes fixed upon the ash-tray of her dead husband.

And then followed his career in the university, and the friendships contracted there, and the poor mother's dejection when she saw that her son was trying his wings. "I exist for you, I for you," she used to say to him, "and you — who knows for what other? Such is the world, Son." The day upon which he received his degree in law his mother took his hand when he arrived home and kissed it with dramatic gravity, saying into his ear, "May your father bless you, my son!"

His mother never went to bed until he had done so, and she left his bedside with a kiss. Hence he never could stay up far into the night. And his mother was the first thing he saw when he woke. And at the table, of anything that he did not eat, neither did she eat.

Now and then they went out together for a walk, and as they walked along together in silence under the sky she was thinking of her dead husband, and he of anything that happened to catch his eye. And she always said the same things to him, everyday things, old-time things, yet always new. Many of them began thus, "When you marry —— "

Whenever they passed a beautiful girl, or a girl at all attractive, Augusto's mother looked at him out of the corner of her eye.

And then came death, that gentle, composed, and unhurried death, without pain, which came in noiselessly, on tiptoe, like a bird of passage, and carried her away in a slow flight one autumn afternoon. She died with her hand in the hand of her son, her eyes fixed upon his eyes. Augusto felt her hand growing cold, and he saw that her eyes had ceased to move. He let her hand go after leaving upon its coldness a warm kiss, and he closed her eyes. He knelt beside the bed and the whole story of those uneventful years passed in review before him and above him.

And here he was now in the Alameda, beneath the warbling of the birds, thinking about Eugenia. And Eugenia was already engaged. "What I fear, my son," his mother used to say, "is when you encounter the first thorn in your path of life." If only she were here to make the first thorn blossom into a rose!

"If my mother were living, she would find a solution for this problem," said Augusto to himself. "It is after all not more difficult than an equation of the second degree. And really, at bottom it's only an equation of the second degree."

A faint moaning, as if from some poor animal, interrupted his soliloquy. He searched about and finally, in the midst of a thicket, he discovered a poor puppy which seemed to be trying to find a way out. "Poor little beggar," he said to himself. "He is just newly born, and they have left him out to die. They hadn't the courage to kill him." And he picked him up.

The little animal was seeking the breast of his mother. Augusto rose and returned home, thinking all the time, "When Eugenia knows this it will be a hard knock for my rival. How fond she will be of the poor little animal! And he's good-looking too, he's good-looking. Poor little beggar, see him lick my hands! —— "

"Bring some milk, Domingo, and bring it at once," he said to the servant the moment the door was opened.

"And so it has occurred to you now to buy a dog, señorito?"

"No, I didn't buy him, Domingo. This dog is not a slave; he's free-born. I found him."

"Ah, yes! he's a foundling."

"We are all foundlings, Domingo. Bring some milk."

He brought the milk and a small sponge to make it easier to suck. Afterwards Augusto had them get a nursing bottle for the puppy, for Orfeo — for thus he baptized him, no one knows why, nor did he himself know.

Thenceforth Orfeo was the confidant of his soliloquies and the recipient of the secret of his love for Eugenia.

"Listen, Orfeo," he said to him quietly, "we have to fight. What do you advise me to do? If only my mother had known you — But you will understand, you'll understand, when you sleep in the lap of Eugenia with her soft and gentle hand resting upon you. And now, what are we going to do, Orfeo?"

His lunch of that day was melancholy; melancholy his afternoon walk; his game of chess was melancholy; and melancholy the dreams of the night.

VI

I MUST come to some decision," said
Augusto to himself as he walked up and down in
front of the house numbered 58 in the Avenida de
la Alameda. "This can't go on as it is."

At that moment one of the balconies on the
second floor, where Eugenia lived, was opened, and
there appeared a spare, grey-haired lady with a
bird-cage in her hand, preparing to hang the canary out in the sun. But as she was doing so she
missed the nail and the cage fell to the ground. She
uttered a cry of despair. "Alas, my Pichín!" Augusto rushed to pick up the cage. The poor canary
fluttered about in fright inside of it.

Augusto mounted the stairs, with the canary
in agitation within the cage and his heart in agitation within his breast. The señora was waiting
for him.

"Oh, many thanks, sir!"

"The thanks are due to you, señora."

"My Pichín! My Pichinito! Come, be quiet!
Won't you please walk in, sir?"

"With great pleasure, señora."

And Augusto stepped in.

The señora led him to the drawing-room, and left him alone, saying, "Wait a moment, I am going to put Pichín away."

At this moment an elderly gentleman entered the room, without doubt Eugenia's uncle. He wore smoked glasses and a fez on his head. He approached Augusto and taking a seat near him he said something in Esperanto which meant:

"Do you not believe with me that, thanks to Esperanto, we shall soon have universal peace?"

Augusto thought of flight, but his love for Eugenia restrained him. The other went on talking, and still in Esperanto.

Finally Augusto decided to speak.

"I don't understand a word of what you are saying, my good sir."

"I'll be bound that he was talking to you in that accursed jargon that they call Esperanto," said the aunt just then entering the room. And turning to her husband she said, "Fermín, this is the señor of the canary."

"Well, I don't understand you any better than you understand me when I speak in Esperanto," replied the husband.

"This señor picked up my poor Pichín after he had fallen into the street, and he was kind enough to bring him up to me." And turning to Augusto she asked, "What is your name?"

"Señora, I am Augusto Pérez, son of the late

widow of Pérez Rovira, whom perhaps you may have known."

"Of Doña Soledad?"

"Exactly; of Doña Soledad."

"Oh, I knew the good señora very well. A model of a widow and a mother. I congratulate you upon the fact, señor.

"And I also congratulate myself upon the fact of owing this acquaintance with you to the happy accident of the fall of the canary."

"Happy! Do you call the accident happy?"

"For me, yes."

"Thank you, sir," said Don Fermín, and he added: "Men and their affairs are guided by enigmatical laws, of which nevertheless men can get a glimpse. I, my dear sir, have my own special ideas about nearly everything —— "

"Drop that refrain of yours, husband!" cried the aunt. "And how was it that you were able to run so quickly to the aid of my poor Pichín?"

"I will be frank with you, señora, and make a clean breast of it. I was lingering around the house."

"This house?"

"Yes, señora. You have a charming niece."

"Say no more, sir. Now — now indeed I understand the happy accident. And I see that canaries may be providential.

"Which of us knows the ways of Providence?" said Don Fermín.

"I know them, man, I know them," cried the wife. And turning to Augusto: "The doors of this house are open to you — Well, who would have dreamed it! Son of Doña Soledad! — And in any case you are going to help me rid this girl of a whim that has got into her head."

"And what of her freedom of will?" Don Fermín broke in.

"Hold your tongue, husband, and keep your anarchism to yourself."

"Anarchism!" exclaimed Augusto.

The countenance of Don Fermín was radiant with joy, and in the mildest possible tone he said:

"Yes, my dear sir, I am an anarchist, a mystical anarchist; but theoretically, you understand, only theoretically. Don't be afraid, friend" —— and as he said this he placed his hand in friendly fashion on Augusto's knee. "I don't throw bombs. My anarchism is purely spiritual. For you see, my friend, I have my own ideas about nearly everything."

"And are you an anarchist too?" Augusto asked the aunt, just for something to say.

"I? This is pure nonsense, this idea of nobody giving any orders. If nobody gives any orders who is going to obey? Don't you understand that that is impossible?"

"Oh, men of little faith, who call impossible —— " began Don Fermín.

The aunt interrupted him:

"Very good, my Señor Don Augusto, the bargain is closed. You seem to be an excellent fellow, well-educated, of good family, with an income more than respectable — No, don't thank me. From now on you are my candidate."

"It is a great honour, señora! ——"

"Yes, we must make this young woman see reason. She's not a bad sort, you understand, but she likes to have her own way. And then she was so badly spoiled in the bringing up! — When that terrible catastrophe came upon us in connection with my poor brother —— "

"Catastrophe?" asked Augusto.

"Yes, and since it is a matter of public knowledge, there is no reason why I should conceal it from you. Eugenia's father committed suicide after a most unfortunate speculation in the stock-market, leaving her almost destitute. A house remained to her, but loaded with a mortgage that consumes all of her income. And the poor child has undertaken to go on saving out of her earnings until she gathers enough to lift the mortgage. Just think of it! She couldn't do it if she gave piano-lessons for sixty years!"

At once a generous and heroic purpose was formed in the mind of Augusto.

"The girl is not a bad sort," continued the aunt, "but there is no way of understanding her."

"If you learned Esperanto ——" began Don Fermín.

"Oh, drop your universal languages! Because we don't understand one another in our own language are you going to bring in another?"

"But don't you think, señora," Augusto asked her, "that it would be a good thing if there were only one language?"

"Just so, just so!" cried Don Fermín delightedly.

"Yes, señor," affirmed the aunt positively. "Only one language, and that the Castilian; and then at most the dialect to use with servants who are not rational beings."

Eugenia's aunt was an Asturian, and had a servant, also an Asturian, with whom she quarrelled in the Asturian dialect.

"Now, if we are speaking only theoretically," she continued, "I don't think it is a bad thing to have only one language. For this husband of mine is theoretically almost an enemy of marriage ——"

"Señores," said Augusto rising, "I fear I may be disturbing you ——"

"Oh, you never disturb us, sir," replied the aunt, "and it is understood that we shall see you again. And you know of course that you are my candidate."

As Augusto was going out Don Fermín approached him for a moment and said in his ear, "Don't cherish any idea of that!"

"And why not?" asked Augusto.

"Well, there are presentiments, sir, presentiments."

As he took his leave the last words of the aunt were, "And of course you know that you are my candidate."

When Eugenia returned home her aunt's first words when she saw her were:

"Do you know who has been here, Eugenia? Don Augusto Pérez."

"Augusto Pérez — Augusto Pérez —— Ah, yes! Who brought him here?"

"Pichín, my canary."

"And what did he come for?"

"What a question! He came on your account."

"On my account and brought by a canary? Well, I don't understand. It would be better if you spoke in Esperanto, like Uncle Fermín."

"He comes on your account; and he is a young bachelor, not bad looking, well set up, well educated, clever, and above all rich, dear girl — above all, rich."

"Well, let him keep his riches! Because I work for my living it is not with any idea of selling myself."

"And who said anything to you about selling yourself, you tinder-box?"

"Very well, Aunt, we've said enough. Let's drop this nonsense."

"You'll see him, child, you'll see him, and then you'll be changing your ideas."

"As for that ——— "

"No one can ever say, I will not drink of this water."

"The ways of Providence are mysterious," exclaimed Don Fermín. "God ——— "

"But, man!" his wife turned on him. "How does this talk about God go with your anarchism? I've said it a thousand times. If no one ought to command, what do you mean by talking about God?"

"My anarchism, wife, as you have heard me say another thousand times, is mystical; it is a spiritual anarchism. God does not command as men command. God is also an anarchist. God does not command, but ——— "

"Obeys. Isn't that what you mean?"

"You have said it, wife, you have said it. God himself has enlightened you. Come here!"

He grasped his wife, looked her in the face, blew upon her curls of white hair, and then added:

"He himself has inspired you. Yes, God obeys — obeys ——— "

"Yes, theoretically — isn't that so? And you,

Eugenia, stop your nonsense now and remember that you have a great match offered you."

"But I am an anarchist too, Aunt, only not like Uncle Fermín — not a mystical anarchist."

"Very well, we shall see," the aunt concluded.

VII

OH, Orfeo!" — Augusto was at home talking to Orfeo while he gave him his milk. "Oh, Orfeo! I have taken the important step, the decisive step; I have entered her home, Orfeo, I have entered the sanctuary. Do you know what it is to take a decisive step? The winds of fortune drive us along and all of our steps are decisive. Our steps? But are these steps ours? We are travelling through a wild and tangled forest, Orfeo, in which there are no trails. We make the trails ourselves with our feet as we go along at random. There are persons who think they are following their star; I am following a double star, a twin star. And this star is only the projection of the trail upon the sky — the projection of chance.

"A decisive step! But tell me, Orfeo, what necessity is there that God should be, or the world, or anything whatever? Why does there need to be anything? Doesn't it seem to you that this idea of necessity is nothing but the highest form that chance takes in our minds?

"How did Eugenia come to be here? Is she my creation or am I hers? Or are we two mutual creations, she creating me and I creating her? Can't you say, perhaps, that the whole world is the creation of each thing and each thing the creation of the world? And what is creation? What are you, Orfeo? And what am I?

"It has often occurred to me, Orfeo, to suppose that I did not exist, and I have gone along the street cherishing the idea that other persons did not see me. And at other times I have fancied that they did not see me as I saw myself; and that, while I thought that I was acting soberly and circumspectly, I was really playing the clown without knowing it, and the other people were all laughing at me and mocking me. Hasn't this ever happened to you too, Orfeo? And yet, no; for you are still young and without experience in life. And besides you are only a dog.

"But tell me, Orfeo: there have been men who believed themselves to be dogs; have there ever been dogs that believed themselves to be men?

"What a life is this life of mine, Orfeo, what a life — especially since my mother died! Every hour reaches me because the hours before have thrust it upon me. I have never known what it is to look forward to a future. And now that I begin to get a glimpse of the future, for me it seems to be on the point of turning itself into a past. Eugenia herself is now almost a memory. These fleeting days — this day, this eternal day that is ever passing — gliding away in the mist of tedium. Today like yesterday, tomorrow like today. Look here, Orfeo, these are the ashes that my father left in this ash-tray ——

"This is the revelation of eternity, Orfeo, of terrible eternity. When a man is left alone and closes his eyes to the future — to illusion — he sees before him the awful abyss of eternity. Eternity is not future. When we die, death turns us right-about face in our orbit and we start to march towards the rear, towards the past, towards that which was. And so we go on without end, rewinding the skein of our destiny, and undoing all that infinity of creation which through an eternity has been making us what we are; and we journey towards the nothing without ever reaching it, because it never was.

"Beneath the current of our existence, and within it, there is another current flowing in the opposite direction. In this life we go from yesterday to tomorrow, but there, we go from tomorrow to yesterday. The web of life is being woven and un-ravelled at the same time. And from time to time we get breaths and vapours and even mysterious murmurs from that other world, from that interior of our own world. The inner heart of history is a counter-history; it is a process which inverts the course of history. That subterranean river flows from the sea back to its source.

"Shining now in the heaven of my solitude are

the two eyes of Eugenia. They shine with the glitter of my mother's tears. And they make me believe that I exist — sweet illusion! *Amo, ergo sum.* This love, Orfeo, is like a beneficent rain that dissipates and at the same time condenses the mist of existence. Thanks to love, I feel my soul taking solid form, I touch it. Thanks to love, Orfeo, my soul is beginning to pain me in its very marrow. And the soul itself, what is it but love? What but incarnate pain?

"The days come and go and love abides. There within, very far within, in the very heart of things, the current of this world is rubbing and grinding against the opposite current of that other world, and from this chafing and grinding comes the saddest and sweetest of pains, the pain of living.

"Look at the threads, Orfeo; look at the warp; and see how the thread of the woof goes back and forth with the throw of the shuttle; and watch the play of the treadle as it goes up and down! But tell me, where is the beam upon which is rolled up the texture of our existence — where?"

Inasmuch as Orfeo had never seen a loom, it is very unlikely that he understood his master. But looking into the master's eyes as he spoke, he divined the nature of his feeling.

VIII

*A*UGUSTO was trembling, and he felt, as he sat there, as if he were being stretched upon a rack; and there came upon him a mad desire to jump to his feet, walk about the room, make passes with his hands in the air, play the clown, cry out, and forget that he existed. Neither the presence of Doña Ermelinda, the aunt of Eugenia, nor that of her husband, Don Fermín, the theoretical and mystical anarchist, was sufficient to bring him down to reality.

"Yes, Don Augusto," Doña Ermelinda was saying, "I think it would be better for you to wait; for she can't be very long in coming now. I'll send for her, and then you can see each other and become acquainted; and that is the first step. All matters of this kind have to begin by getting acquainted, isn't that so?"

"To be sure, señora," said Augusto, speaking as if from another world. "The first step is to see each other and get acquainted."

"And I think that as soon as she knows you, well — the rest is clear."

"Not so very clear," objected Don Fermín.

"The ways of Providence are mysterious always —
And as for this idea that, in order to be married,
it is first necessary, or even convenient, to know
each other, I disagree — I disagree. The only effec-
tive knowledge is that which comes *post nuptias.*
You have heard me explain before, my dear, what
knowing signifies in the language of the Bible.
And believe me, there is no other knowledge
more real and essential than that, no knowledge
more —— "

"Hold your tongue, sir, hold your tongue and
don't talk like a fool."

"Knowledge, Ermelinda —— "

The door-bell rang.

"There she is!" cried the uncle in a tone of
mystery.

Augusto felt a wave of fire rising within him
from the floor and passing upwards through his
head until it was lost in the space above him. And
his heart began to beat his breast like a hammer
beating an anvil.

They heard the door open, and then the sound
of footsteps, rapid, even, and rhythmical. Without knowing why, Augusto felt himself growing
calmer.

"I am going to call her," said Don Fermín,
about to rise from his seat.

"No, no, don't!" cried Doña Ermelinda; and
she called the servant.

When the servant appeared she said, "Ask
Señorita Eugenia if she will come in here."

A deep silence followed. Like so many con-
spirators, none of them ventured to speak. And
Augusto kept saying to himself, "Shall I be able
to stand it? When her eyes fill the space of that
doorway shall I not turn as red as a poppy or white
as a lily? Won't my heart burst?"

A slight rustle was heard as of a dove setting
out on a flight, an "Ah!" short and dry, and the
eyes of Eugenia, set in a face full of the freshness
of life, above a body which hardly seemed to rest
upon the floor, appeared on the scene and seemed
to shed upon it a new and mysterious spiritual
light. And Augusto felt himself to be quite calm,
tremendously calm, fixed to his seat as if he were
a plant that had grown there, as if, indeed, he were
some sort of vegetable, unconscious of himself and
absorbed in the mysterious spiritual light radiating
from those eyes. And it was only when he heard
Doña Ermelinda say, "Here is our friend Don
Augusto Pérez," that he returned to himself and
rose to his feet with an attempt to smile.

"This is our friend Don Augusto Pérez, who
wishes to make your acquaintance."

"The canary-man?"

"Yes, the canary-man, señorita," replied Augusto, approaching her and extending his hand.
And he thought, "She will burn me with hers."

He was mistaken. A hand white and cold —
white as snow and, like the snow, cold — touched
his own. And Augusto felt a kind of fluid serenity
permeating his whole being.

Eugenia took a seat.

"And this kind sir —— " the pianist began.

" 'This kind sir' — 'this kind sir' — " passed
rapidly through the mind of Augusto, " 'this kind
sir'! She calls me a kind sir! Rather a bad omen!"

"This kind sir, my daughter, who has by a
happy accident —— "

"Yes, the canary accident."

"The ways of Providence are mysterious!" the
anarchist pronounced.

"This kind sir, I say," continued the aunt,
"who, by a happy accident, has become acquainted
with us, and who turns out to be the son of a
lady with whom I had some acquaintance, and
whom I respected greatly — this kind sir, being
now a friend of the family, wishes to make your acquaintance, Eugenia."

"And to express his admiration for her," added
added Augusto.

"Admiration?" exclaimed Eugenia.

"Yes, as a pianist."

"Ah, really!"

"Señorita, I know your great love of
art —— "

"Art? What art — the art of music?"

"Of course!"

"Then they have misinformed you, Don Augusto."

" 'Don Augusto'! 'Don Augusto'!" he thought. "Don! — What a bad omen, this 'Don'! Almost as bad as that 'kind sir'!" And then aloud:

"Are you not fond of music?"

"Not a bit, I assure you."

"Liduvina is right," thought Augusto. "After she is married, if her husband can support her, she will never touch the keys of a piano again." And then aloud:

"Since you are known to be such an excellent teacher —— "

"I try to fulfil my professional duties as well as I can; and now that I have to earn my own living —— "

"This idea of having to earn your own living —— " began Don Fermín.

"Very well, that will do," interrupted the aunt. "Señor Don Augusto has already been informed about everything —— "

"About everything? About what?" asked Eugenia with asperity, and with a slight movement towards rising from her seat.

"Yes, about the matter of the mortgage —— "

"How is that?" exclaimed the niece jumping to her feet. "But what is this, what is the meaning of it all, what is the purpose of this visit?"

"I have already told you, my dear, that this señor wishes to make your acquaintance. And please don't get so excited."

"But there are some things that —— "

"Please excuse your aunt, señorita," begged Augusto rising also to his feet, as the aunt and uncle did the same, "but it has been only — And as for that matter of the mortgage and of your own self-denial and love of work, I have made no attempt to extort this very interesting information from the señora, your aunt; I —— "

"Yes, you confined yourself to bringing in the canary, a few days after having sent me a letter."

"I did, I will not deny it."

"Well, then, kind sir, I will return the answer to that letter when it pleases me to do so, and not at anyone's dictation. And now I had better withdraw."

"Good! Good!" cried Don Fermín. "This shows firmness and independence! This is the woman of the future! Women of this kind have to be won with the fist, friend Pérez, with the fist!"

"Señorita —— !" begged Augusto, approaching her.

"I beg your pardon," said Eugenia; and in tak-

ing leave of him she gave him her hand, white and
cold as before — and as the snow.

As she turned to leave the room, and as those
eyes that were the source of the mysterious spiritual light, thus disappeared, Augusto felt the wave
of fire running through his body again; his heart
beat his breast like a hammer beating an anvil; and
his head seemed ready to burst.

"Are you feeling ill?" Don Fermín asked him.

"What a child! O Lord, what a child!" cried
Doña Ermelinda.

"Splendid! Majestic! Heroic! A woman — the
full stature of a woman!" Augusto was saying.

"I think so too," added the uncle.

"Forgive her, Señor Don Augusto," the aunt
continued, "forgive her. This girl is a young por-
cupine. Who could have thought it?"

"Oh, but I am delighted with her, señora, delighted! Really, this robust independence of character — in which I myself am so deficient — is
just what most arouses my enthusiasm. It is certainly she, she and not any other woman, whom I
need."

"Yes, Señor Pérez, yes," declaimed the anarchist. "This is the woman of the future!"

"And what am I?" demanded Doña Ermelinda.

"You? You are the woman of the past. But
she, I say, is the woman of the future! Clearly it is

not for nothing that she has been listening to me,
one day and another, discoursing upon the future
of society and upon the woman of the future! Not
in vain have I inculcated in her the emancipating
doctrines of anarchism — without bombs!"

"Well, it is my opinion," said the aunt crossly,
"that this girl is quite capable of throwing bombs."

"And even if it were so —— " interposed Augusto.

"Never! Never!" cried the uncle.

"But what of it?"

"Don Augusto! Don Augusto!"

"I think," added the aunt, "that you should
not let what has just happened persuade you to
withdraw your suit."

"Certainly not. This only makes it the more
worth while."

"On to the conquest, then! And of course
you know that we are on your side, and that you
can come to this house of yours as often as you
wish, whether it suits Eugenia or not."

"But, wife, surely she has not said that Don
Augusto's visits here are displeasing to her! You'll
have to win her with the fist, friend, with the fist!
You will be coming to know her now, and you
will see of what fine temper she is. This is the full
stature of a woman, Don Augusto, and you'll have
to win her with the fist, with the fist. Didn't you
want to know her?"

"Yes, but —— "

"Of course, of course! On to the contest, then, my friend!"

"Certainly, by all means. And now good-bye."

Don Fermín then took Augusto apart to say this to him:

"I forgot to tell you that when you write to Eugenia be sure to write her name with a *j*, and not with a *g*, Eujenia; and del Arco with a *k*: Eujenia Domingo del Ar*k*o."

"But why?"

"Because until the happy day arrives when Esperanto is to be the only language — one language for all humanity! — we must write the Castilian with phonetic spelling. No more *c's!* Down with the *c! Za, ze zi, zo, zu,* with *z,* and *ka, ke, ki, ko, ku,* with *k.* And down with *h's.* The *h* is absurd, reactionary, authoritarian, mediæval, and retrogressive! Down with *h!*"

"And so you are also a phoneticist?"

"Also? Why 'also'?"

"Because you are already an anarchist and an Esperantist."

"It is all one, señor, all one. Anarchism, Esperantism, spiritism, vegetarianism, phoneticism — it's all one! Down with authority! Down with the division of tongues! Down with vile matter and with death! Down with meat! Down with the *h!* Good-bye."

They parted, and Augusto went out into the street feeling as if he had been lightened of a great weight, and even feeling joyous. He would never have guessed beforehand at what was now passing in his soul. Eugenia's manner of presenting herself the first time they had seen each other quietly and close at hand and had talked to one another, this, so far from paining him, only inflamed him the more and stimulated his courage. The world seemed to him bigger, the air purer, the sky bluer. It was as if he were for the first time really breathing. In his innermost ear that word of his mother's was singing, Marry! Nearly all the women that he passed on the street seemed pretty, many of them beautiful, and not one of them ugly. To him it seemed that the world was beginning to be illuminated by a new mysterious light, proceeding from two great invisible stars shining beyond the blue of the sky, above the dome of the heavens. He was beginning to know the world. And without even guessing how he came to the idea, he set himself to reflect upon the very deep source of that common tendency to associate the sin of the flesh with the fall of our first parents, for having tasted of the fruit of the tree of knowledge of good and evil.

And he meditated upon the doctrine of Don Fermín regarding the origin of knowledge.

When he arrived home and Orfeo ran out to welcome him, he took him up into his arms and said: "Today we begin a new life, Orfeo. Don't you feel that the world is bigger, the air purer, the sky bluer? Ah, when you see her, Orfeo, when you know her! — Then you will feel the woe of being only a dog, just as I feel the woe of being only a man! And tell me, Orfeo, how do you dogs ever know anything if you don't sin — if your knowledge is not sin? Knowledge that is not sin is not what you call knowledge, it is not rational."

When his faithful Liduvina served his dinner she stood there for a moment looking at him.

"Why are you looking at me?" asked Augusto.

"It seems to me there has been a change."

"What makes you think so?"

"The señorito has a different expression."

"Do you think so?"

"It's plain enough. And tell me, how are you getting on with the piano-teacher?"

"Liduvina! Liduvina!"

"I beg your pardon, señorito. But I am so much concerned for your happiness."

"Who knows what that is?"

"True."

And the two of them gazed at the floor as if the secret of happiness lay beneath it.

IX

T H E next day Eugenia was confer-
ring with a young gentleman in the rather narrow
quarters of a doorman's box, the *concierge* having
discreetly retired to take the air at the door of the
house.

"This will have to stop, Mauricio," Eugenia
was saying. "We can't go on in this way, especially
after what I told you happened yesterday."

"But didn't you say," said the person addressed as Mauricio, "that this admirer of yours is
a poor noodle who goes about with his head in the
clouds?"

"Yes, but he has money, and my aunt is not
going to leave me in peace. And the fact is, I don't
care to make myself unpleasant to anybody; but
neither do I want them to give me a headache."

"Send him off!"

"Send him off? Where from — from my uncle's house? Suppose they object?"

"Don't bother about him."

"I am not bothering about him, and I don't
expect to, but I think that the poor fellow is likely

to form the habit of coming when I am at home. There's no point, you understand, in simply shutting myself in my room and refusing to let him see me. He's going to dedicate himself to a martyrdom of silence, without making any demands upon me."

"Then let him dedicate himself."

"No, I can't resist any kind of a beggar, and least of all those who beg for alms with their eyes. And if you saw how he looks at me!"

"Does he make you feel tenderly towards him?"

"He worries me. And the truth is — why shouldn't I tell you? — yes, he does make me feel tenderly towards him."

"And you are afraid?"

"Boy, don't be stupid! I am not afraid of anything. There's nobody for me but you."

"I was sure of that," replied Mauricio, full of conviction, and placing his hand on Eugenia's knee, he left it there.

"You will have to make up your mind, Mauricio."

"To what, sweetheart, to what?"

"To what? To what do you suppose, man? To our being married at once!"

"And what are we going to live on?"

"On my work, until you find something to do."

"On your work?"

"Yes, on the detestable music!"

"On your work? Most certainly not! Never! Never! Never! Anything rather than that I should live on your work! I'll look for something, and keep on looking, and meanwhile we'll wait ———— "

"We'll wait — and wait — and so the years will slip by us!" exclaimed Eugenia, tapping upon the floor with the foot belonging to the knee upon which Mauricio was resting his hand.

He, feeling his hand thus rudely shaken, took it away from where it was perched, but only to put his arm about his fiancée's neck while with his fingers he played with one of her ear-rings. She allowed him to do it.

"Listen, Eugenia, just for the fun of it you may make yourself agreeable to this noodle, if you like."

"Mauricio!"

"I beg your pardon. Don't be offended, sweetheart!" And bending his arm he brought Eugenia's head close to his own, sought her lips with his, and, closing his eyes, united them in a long, silent, and moist kiss.

"Mauricio!"

Then he kissed her upon her eyes.

"This can't go on, Mauricio!"

"Why not? Is there anything nicer? Do you think we shall ever have a better time?"

"I tell you, Mauricio, that it can't go on. You will have to find work. I hate the music."

The poor child felt obscurely, with knowing clearly why, that music is an eternal preparation, a preparation for an event that never comes to pass, an eternal beginning that leads to nothing. She had had enough of the music.

"I'll look for work, Eugenia, I'll look for work."

"You are always saying the same thing and we are always in the same old place."

"Do you suppose ——"

"The fact is, I *know* that at bottom you are nothing but a loafer, and that it is going to be necessary for me to find work for you. Naturally — since for you men it costs nothing to wait —— !"

"You may think so ——"

"Yes, yes, I know what I am talking about. And so I tell you again, I don't wish to see the pleading eyes of the Señorito Don Augusto, eyes like those of a starving puppy ——"

"What ideas you have, girl!"

"And now," she added, rising and at the same time removing his hand, "be quiet for a while and then get some fresh air. You need it badly."

"Eugenia! Eugenia!" he sighed, speaking into her ear in a tone dry and feverish. "If you loved ——"

"It is you who need to learn to love, Mauricio. And so — be a man! Look for work and make up your mind soon; if you don't find it, I shall do the work. But make up your mind soon. And if you let it go —— "

"If I let it go, then what?"

"Then nothing at all! We shall have to put an end to this!"

And without giving him a chance to reply she left the porter's box. As she passed the *concierge* she said:

"Your nephew is still here, Señora Marta. Tell him to make up his mind at once."

And Eugenia went out into street holding her head high. Just at that moment a hand-organ was beginning a maddening polka. "Oh, horrors! horrors! horrors!" said the girl to herself, and she fled, rather than walked, down the street.

x

On the day after his visit to Eugenia's
house, and at the very time when she was putting
the spurs into the amorous content of her lover in
the doorman's box, Augusto, feeling the need of a
confidant, set out to see his chum Victor.

Augusto felt like a different man. It was
as if that visit and its revelation of the valiant
woman — strength streamed from her eyes — had
ploughed up the very depths of his soul, exposing
there a spring which until then had been hidden.
His step was firmer, he breathed more freely.

"Now I have an objective, a purpose in this
life of mine," he said to himself, "and it is to con-
quer this girl or be conquered by her. And it's all
the same thing. In love it is the same thing to con-
quer and to be conquered. And yet, no — no! To
be conquered means here that she abandons me
for the other. For the other, yes, because there is
beyond doubt another. Another? Another what? Is
it certain that I am one of them? I am suing and
soliciting, but the other — the other, it occurs to
me, is neither suing nor soliciting; and he is neither
suing nor soliciting because he has already obtained

— of course nothing more than the love of the sweet Eugenia. But nothing more? —— "

A feminine body passing close to him, radiant with the freshness and joy of health, interrupted his soliloquy and carried him along in its train. Almost mechanically he set out to follow that body while continuing his soliloquy.

"And how beautiful she is! Both this one and that, the one and the other. And perhaps the other man, instead of suing and soliciting, is being sued and solicited; perhaps he fails to respond to her as she deserves —— But what a delight this girl is! And how gracefully she is greeting the man over there! Where can she have got those eyes? They are very nearly the same as those other eyes — Eugenia's. What a delicious pleasure it must be to forget life and death in those arms! To let yourself be rocked in them as upon waves of flesh! The other man! —— But the real other is not Eugenia's fiancé, he's not that man that she loves; I am the real other. Yes, I am the other; I am another."

Just as he reached this conclusion, that he was another, the young woman that he was following entered a house. Augusto stopped short and looked at the house. And then it was brought home to him that he had come there by following her. Thereupon he recalled the fact that he had set out to go to the Casino, and he turned in that direction. And he continued:

"But, Lord, what a lot of beautiful women there are in the world! Nearly all are beautiful. Thanks, O Lord, thanks to thee, *gratias agimus tibi propter magnam gloriam tuam,* we give thanks to thee for thy great glory! Thy glory is the beauty of woman, O Lord! But what a head of hair, Lord, what hair!"

It was indeed a glorious head of hair — that of a servant-maid who passed him just then with a basket on her arm. And he turned to follow her. The light seemed to nest in the gold of that hair, and it seemed as if the hair was struggling to break loose from its braids and to scatter itself into the fresh, clear air. And beneath the hair a face which was all of it a smile.

"I am another, I am the other," continued Augusto as he followed the girl with the basket. "But may there not be other women? Yes, there are doubtless other women for me if I am the other man! But like the one, like her, like the only one — no one like her, no one! All of these others are merely imitations of her, of the one, the only one — of my sweet Eugenia! Mine? Yes, by my thought and by my desire I have made her mine. He, the other — that is to say, the one — may come to possess her in the material sense, but the mysterious spiritual light of those eyes is mine, mine, mine! But doesn't this golden hair also reflect a mysterious spiritual light? Is there only one Eu-

genia or are there two, one mine and the other that
of her lover? Well, if this is the case, if there are
two, let him keep his and I will keep mine. When
sadness comes to visit me, as it does so often at
night; when there comes upon me the desire to
weep without knowing why; oh, how sweet it is
going to be to cover my head, my mouth, my
eyes, with this golden hair and to breathe the
air that comes through it filtered and perfumed!
But —— "

He felt himself suddenly halted. The girl with
the basket had stopped to talk to a friend. Augusto
hesitated a moment, and then, saying to himself,
"Bah, there are so many beautiful women since I
have known Eugenia!" he resumed his walk, turning in the direction of the Casino.

"If she insists upon choosing the other — that
is to say, the one — I am capable of a heroic resolution, something that is going to astonish by its
magnanimity. In any case, whether she loves me or
not, this matter of the mortgage can't remain
where it is."

He was startled out of his soliloquy by an explosion of joy that seemed to spring from the clear
sky. A couple of girls near him were laughing, and
their laughter was like the warbling of birds in an
arbour of flowers. He fixed his beauty-thirsting
eyes for a moment upon that pair of girls, and they
seemed to him a single twin body; they were walk-

ing arm in arm. And there came upon him a mad impulse to stop them, to take an arm of each and, placing himself between them, to go along with them, looking up into the heavens, whithersoever the winds of life might take them.

"But how many beautiful women there have been since I met Eugenia!" he said to himself, meanwhile following that laughing pair. "This world has been converted into a paradise! What eyes! What hair! What laughter! One is blonde and the other brunette. But which is the blonde? And which is the brunette? I've got them confused, one with the other! —— "

"But, old fellow, are you awake or are you walking in your sleep?"

"Hullo, Victor."

"I was expecting you at the Casino, and when you didn't come —— "

"I was on my way there."

"On your way? And in this direction? Are you mad?"

"True. I beg your pardon. But listen, now I am going to tell you the truth. I think I spoke to you of Eugenia —— "

"Of the piano-teacher? Yes."

"Well, then, I am madly in love with her; like a —— "

"Yes, like one who is in love. Go on."

"I am mad, my boy, mad. Yesterday I saw her in her home, on the pretext of calling upon her aunt and uncle; I saw her —— "

"And she looked at you, didn't she? And you believed in God?"

"No, she didn't look at me, she enveloped me in her gaze; and I didn't believe in God, I believed that I was a god."

"She's hit you hard, my boy."

"And in spite of her lordly airs too! But I don't know what has come over me since. Nearly all the women I see look beautiful, and since I left home, certainly not more than half an hour ago, I have already fallen in love with three — no, with four; with one who was all eyes, and then with a glorious head of hair, and just a few minutes ago with a pair, one fair and the other dark, who were laughing like the angels. And I followed all four of them. What do you make of it?"

"Why, the meaning of it is, my dear Augusto, that your stock of love was lying dormant at the bottom of your soul with no means of getting into life. Eugenia, the piano-teacher, came along, she shook you and stirred up with her eyes the pool in which your love was sleeping; the love awoke, it found its source in her, but since you have so much love, it is spreading now in all directions. When a man like you truly falls in love with one woman, he falls in love with all the others at the same time."

"But I thought it would be just the opposite. But, by the way, look at that girl with the dark hair! She is night made into day! It is quite right to say that black is the colour that absorbs the most light! Don't you get the feeling of the light hidden beneath her hair, and beneath the jet of her eyes? Let's follow her."

"Just as you like."

"Why yes, I thought it would be just the opposite; and that when a man really falls in love, then his love is concentrated upon one only, rather than poured over all; and that all the rest of the women will then be as nothing and of no interest —— But look, see that glint of the sun in the blackness of her hair!"

"No; you'll see how it is — you'll see, if I succeed in explaining it to you. You were already in love, without knowing it of course, with woman in the abstract, and not with this woman or that. When you saw Eugenia that abstract became concrete, and woman became one woman, and you fell in love with her. And now you are passing over from her, but without leaving her, to nearly all women, and you are falling in love with the collective woman, with the genus. You have passed, then, from the abstract to the concrete and from the concrete to the generic; from woman to one woman and from one woman to woman."

"But I say, now you're talking metaphysics!"

"And what is love but metaphysics?"

"Humph!"

"And in your case especially. For your being in love is all of it purely cerebral; or as we say, in your head."

"Doubtless that is what you think —— " exclaimed Augusto rather crossly. For he was a little bit piqued. The idea that his being in love was only in his head had gone to the depths of his soul, and it hurt him.

"And if you drive me to it, I will tell you that you yourself are nothing but a pure idea, an entity of fiction —— "

"Do you mean that you don't believe me capable of being really in love, like other men?"

"You are really in love; I am sure of that; but in your head only. You think that you are in love —— "

"And what else is there to being in love besides thinking that it is so?"

"Ah, my dear fellow, that is more complicated than you imagine!"

"Tell me, how do you know that a man is really in love and does not merely think it to be so?"

"Look here, it would be better to leave this subject and talk about something else."

When Augusto returned home he took Orfeo in his arms and said to him: "Let's see, Orfeo, how

does being in love differ from merely thinking it?
Am I or am I not in love with Eugenia? Is it true
that when I see her, my heart does not thump in
my breast and my blood is not on fire? Is it true
that I am not like other men? I shall have to show
them, Orfeo, that I am just as good as they are!"

At supper-time he turned to Liduvina and
asked her:

"Tell me, Liduvina, how do you know when
a man is really in love?"

"But what strange ideas you have, señorito!"

"Come, tell me, how do you know?"

"Well, you know it — you know it when he
says and does a lot of foolish things. When a man
really falls in love with a woman — is gone on
her, as we say — he ceases to be a man —— "

"But what is he then?"

"He is — he is — he's a thing, a sort of animal. A woman can do with him anything she
pleases."

"Then when a woman really falls in love with
a man, and is gone on him, as you say, can the man
do anything that he pleases with her?"

"That isn't quite the same thing —— "

"Why not, why not?"

"That is very hard to explain, señorito. But are
you really in love?"

"That is what I am trying to find out. But
as for saying and doing foolish things, things of any

consequence, I don't think I have done any of them yet — so at least it seems to me —— "

Liduvina was silent, and Augusto asked himself, "Can it be that I am not really in love?"

XI

WHEN Augusto called again at the house of Don Fermín and Doña Ermelinda, the maid led him to the drawing-room, saying, "I'll announce you." He remained for a few moments alone, with the sense of being in a void. Deep within his breast he felt a weight of oppression. A sensation of torturing solemnity seemed to bind and suffocate him. He sat down only to rise again; and he occupied the time by looking at the pictures hung on the wall, among them a portrait of Eugenia. He had an impulse to break into a run and escape. Presently, hearing some light footsteps, he felt a dagger of ice piercing his breast, and something like a fog penetrating his head. The door of the room opened and Eugenia appeared. The poor fellow clung for support to the arm of a chair. She, noting his pallor, turned pale for a moment and stood still in the middle of the room, and then, approaching him, she said in a low, dry tone:

"What is the matter, Don Augusto, are you ill?"

"No, it's nothing; nothing of any consequence ——"

"Do you wish anything? Is there anything I can bring you?"

"A glass of water."

Eugenia, seizing upon this as a way of doing something, left the room herself to get the glass of water and brought it in at once. The water trembled in the glass, but the glass trembled more in the hands of Augusto, who drank it precipitously in one gulp, spilling the water over his chin, all the while keeping his eyes fixed upon the eyes of Eugenia.

"If you wish," she said, "I will have them make you a cup of tea, or bring you perhaps some camomile-tea, or some linden-tea —— What was the matter?"

"Oh, nothing. No, it was nothing. Thanks, Eugenia, thanks!" — and he wiped the water from his chin.

"Very well, and now take a seat." And when they were seated she proceeded, "I was expecting you to call some time soon, and I told the maid that even if my aunt and uncle should be out, as they sometimes are in the afternoon, she should show you in and then call me. In any case I wanted to talk to you alone."

"Oh, Eugenia, Eugenia!"

"Yes, but let us take things more coolly. I never thought that you would take it so much to heart. You alarmed me when I came in; you looked like a dead man."

"And I was really more dead than alive."

"It is going to be necessary for us to come to an understanding."

"Eugenia!" exclaimed the poor fellow. He held out his hand but drew it back at once.

"It seems that you are not yet in a state in which we can talk quietly, like good friends. Let me see!" And she took his hand to feel his pulse.

Poor Augusto's pulse began to beat feverishly; he turned red and his face burned. Eugenia's eyes were blotted out of sight, and he no longer saw anything but mist — a red mist. For a moment he feared he might lose consciousness.

"Have pity, Eugenia, have pity on me!"

"Control yourself, Don Augusto, control yourself."

"Don Augusto — Don Augusto — Don — Don —— "

"Yes, my good Don Augusto, control yourself and let us talk quietly."

"But, permit me —— " and he took between his two hands that right hand, cold and white as the snow, with tapering fingers, made for caressing the keys of the piano and drawing from them sweet arpeggios.

"Just as you like, Don Augusto."

He raised the hand to his lips and covered it with kisses — which did little to moderate its white coolness.

"When you have finished, Don Augusto, we'll begin to talk."

"But listen, Eugenia, wait —— "

"No, no, no, behave yourself!" And taking her hand out of his, she proceeded: "I don't know what sort of expectations my aunt and uncle have led you to form — or rather my aunt; but it seems to be the case that they have misled you."

"Misled me —how?"

"Yes, they ought to have told you that I am engaged."

"I know it."

"Did they tell you?"

"No, nobody told me, but I know it."

"Then —— "

"But the fact is, Eugenia, that I claim nothing, I am looking for nothing, I ask for nothing; I am content, Eugenia, to be allowed to come now and then and bathe my soul in the glances of these eyes, intoxicate myself in the vapour of your breath —— "

"Come now, Don Augusto, these are the kind of things that you read in books; let's drop that. I have no objection to your coming as often as you wish. You may see me and see me again, and you may talk with me, and you may even — you have seen already that you may even kiss my hand. But I have a fiancé, with whom I am in love, and whom I expect to marry."

"But are you really in love with him?"

"What a question!"

"And just how do you know that you are in love with him?"

"But can it be that you have gone mad, Don Augusto?"

"No, no; I ask you the question because my best friend has told me that there are many persons who think they are in love without really being so."

"He said that about you, didn't he?"

"Yes, he said it about me. But what of it?"

"Because in your case it may be true."

"But do you think, Eugenia, do you think that I am not really in love with you?"

"Not so loud, Don Augusto. The maid will hear you."

"Yes, yes," he went on, becoming more and more excited, "there are some people who think that I am incapable of being really in love —— "

"Excuse me a moment," Eugenia interrupted, and she went out, leaving him alone.

Presently she returned and with the utmost tranquillity she said to him:

"How is it, Don Augusto? Have you calmed down?"

"Eugenia! Eugenia!"

Just then a knock was heard at the front door, and Eugenia said, "My Aunt and uncle!" A few moments later they entered the drawing-room.

"Don Augusto came to pay us a visit, and I went myself to open the door. He thought of going away again, but I asked him to come in and told him that you would not be long in coming — and here he is!"

"The time will come," exclaimed Don Fermín, "when all the conventions of society will have vanished. I am convinced that the hedges and walls built around private property serve only as incentives for those whom we call thieves — the real thieves being the others, the proprietors. There is no property so secure as that which has neither hedges nor walls, and is within the reach of everybody. Man is born good, he is good by nature; it is society that perverts and corrupts him."

"Oh, be quiet," exclaimed Doña Ermelinda. "You don't let me hear the canary sing. Don't you hear him, Don Augusto? It is a delight to listen to him. And you should have heard the canary that I had when Eugenia used to practice her lessons on the piano. He became so excited, and the more she hammered the keys the more and the louder he tried to sing. So that in the end he died from it, he burst a —— "

"Even the domestic animals become contaminated by our vices!" continued Don Fermín. "Even the animals that live with us we have uprooted and taken out of the blessed state of nature! Oh, humanity, humanity!"

"Did you have to wait long, Don Augusto?" asked Doña Ermelinda.

"Oh no, señora, no, not at all, a mere instant, brief as a flash of lightning — at least so it seemed to me ———— "

"Ah, indeed."

"Yes, aunt, a very short time, but long enough for him to recover from a slight indisposition which he brought with him from the street ———— "

"How was that?"

"Oh, it was nothing, señora, nothing at all ———— "

"And now I must leave you, I have something to do," said Eugenia, and after shaking hands with Augusto she went out.

"Tell me, how is it coming along?" the aunt asked Augusto as soon as Eugenia had left.

"What do you mean by 'it'?"

"The conquest, of course!"

"Badly, very badly. She tells me that she has a lover and that she is going to marry him."

"Didn't I tell you, Ermelinda, didn't I tell you?"

"No, I say, no, *no!* That shall not be. This matter of the lover is a fit of madness, Don Augusto, madness!"

"But, señora, what if she is in love with him?"

"That is what I say," cried the uncle. "That is what I say. Freedom, sacred freedom, freedom of choice!"

"No, no, no! Do you suppose that this child knows what she is doing? To think of rejecting you, Don Augusto, you! That shall not be!"

"But pause and reflect a moment, señora. One cannot, and one ought not, thus to violate the will of a young woman like Eugenia. It is a matter of her happiness, and it is our duty to think of nothing but that, and even to sacrifice ourselves so that she may have it."

"You, Don Augusto, are you ready to sacrifice yourself?"

"I? Yes, it is for me to do so too, señora! I am ready to sacrifice myself for the happiness of your niece, Eugenia, because my own happiness consists in her being happy!"

"Bravo!" cried the uncle, "Bravo! Bravo! Behold, a hero! Behold, an anarchist — a mystical anarchist!"

"Anarchist?" said Augusto.

"Anarchist, yes. For my anarchism consists in this, and precisely in this, that each shall sacrifice himself for the rest, that each shall be happy in making others happy, that —— "

"And how agreeable you always are, Fermín, when your soup is not served until ten minutes after twelve."

"Yes, but of course you know, Ermelinda, that my anarchism is theoretical. I strive to reach perfection, but —— "

"And happiness is also theoretical!" exclaimed Augusto ruefully, as if speaking to himself, and he continued: "I have decided to sacrifice myself for Eugenia and I have thought of a heroic act."

"What is it?"

"Did you not tell me once, señora, that the house which was left to Eugenia by her unfortunate father —— "

"Yes, my poor brother."

" — is loaded with a mortgage that consumes all of her income?"

'Yes, señor."

"Well, then; I know what I have to do!" And he moved toward the door.

"But, Don Augusto —— "

"Augusto feels himself to be capable of the most heroic decisions and of the greatest sacrifices. And now we shall see whether he is in love only with his head or also with his heart; whether he thinks that he is in love without really being so! Eugenia, señores, has awakened me to life, and no matter whose she may be, I owe her an eternal debt of gratitude. And now, farewell."

He departed solemnly. He had hardly left when Doña Ermelinda shrieked, "Oh, that girl, what an *idiot!*"

XII

"Señorito," Liduvina came in one day to say to Augusto, "here is the girl with the laundry."

"The girl with the laundry? Ah, yes! Let her come in."

She entered carrying a basket with Augusto's clothes. The two stood looking at each other, and the poor girl felt that her face was burning; for in the many times she had come to the house before nothing of that kind had ever happened to her. In the times past it had seemed as if the señorito had not even seen her. This had irritated her and made her even a trifle peevish, for she thought that she knew what was due her. To pay no attention to her! Not to look at her as other men looked at her! Not to devour her with his eyes; nay, to lap hers with his, and her mouth, and whole face!

"What is the matter with you, Rosario? For I think that is your name, isn't it?"

"Yes, that is my name."

"But what is the matter with you?"

"But why, Señorito Augusto?"

"I have never seen you blush as you do to-day. And besides, you seem different."

"It seems to me that it is you who are different."

"Perhaps — perhaps —— But come, come over here!"

"Stop your joking now, and let us get done."

"Joking? But do you think I am joking?" he said in a more serious tone. "Come nearer — that's the way — and let me see you."

"But haven't you often seen me before?"

"Yes, but until now I have never noticed that you were as pretty as you are."

"Come now, señorito, don't laugh at me —— " And her face was on fire.

"And just now especially, with all this colour, like the glow of the sun —— "

"Come now!"

"Come here; come. You are thinking that Señorito Augusto has gone mad, aren't you? But no, it isn't that. No! The fact is that until now he has always been mad, or rather, until now he has been a fool, a fool about everything, lost in a fog, blind. It's only a short time ago that his eyes were opened. You can see for yourself; think of the many times you have been in the house, and he has looked at you and never seen you. It is, Rosario, as if he had not lived — he was a fool, a fool! But what is the matter with you, little girl, what is it that ails you?"

Rosario, who had sunk into a chair, hid her

face in her hands and burst out crying. Augusto rose, closed the door, and turning to the girl put a hand upon her shoulder and said to her in a very low tone, and with more warmth and moisture in his voice, "But what is the matter, child, what is it?"

"When you say things like that, you make me cry, Don Augusto."

"Angel of God!"

"You mustn't say such things, Don Augusto."

"Why shouldn't I say them? Yes, I lived blind and idiotic, as if I had never lived at all, until a woman came — another woman, you understand — and opened my eyes, and I saw the world; and above all I learned to see you, all you women ——— "

"And this woman — she must be a bad woman ——— "

"Bad? You call her bad? Do you know what you are saying, Rosario, do you know what you are saying? Do you know what it is to be bad? What is it to be bad? No, no, this woman is an angel, like you. But this woman doesn't love me — doesn't love me — no, she doesn't love me ——— " And as he said this his voice broke and his eyes were dimmed with tears.

"Poor Don Augusto!"

"Yes, you have said it, Rosario, you have said it. Poor Don Augusto! But listen, Rosario, drop the 'Don' and say 'Poor Augusto'! Come, say it: 'Poor Augusto'!"

"But, señorito —— "

"Come, say it: 'Poor Augusto'!"

"If I must — poor Augusto!"

Augusto sat down.

"Come here!" he said.

She rose like one obeying a hypnotic suggestion, as if she were being moved by clock-work, her breast heaving. He grasped her, seated her on his knees, pressed her violently to his breast, and holding his cheek pressed close to the girl's cheek, which was shedding fire, he burst out with:

"Oh, Rosario, Rosario, I don't know what is happening to me, I don't know what is coming over me! This woman whom you call bad without knowing her, has struck me blind in giving me sight. I was not living, and now I do live; but now that I live is just when I see what it is to die. I must guard myself against this woman, I must guard myself against her eyes. Will you help me, Rosario, will you help to protect me from her?"

The faintest possible "Yes," in a whisper that seemed to come from another world, brushed by the ear of Augusto.

"I don't know now what is the matter with me, Rosario, nor what I say, nor what I do, nor what I think; I don't know whether or not I am

in love with this woman, with this woman that you
call bad —— "

"Don Augusto, I —— "

"Augusto, Augusto —— "

"Augusto, I —— "

"Very well, that will do. Now keep quiet" —
and he closed his eyes. "Don't say a word; let me
talk alone, to myself. It is the way I have lived since
my mother died, by myself, always by myself;
that is to say, always asleep. And I have not known
what it is to sleep together, two sleeping the same
dream. Sleeping together! Not merely being together, each sleeping his own dream; no, sleeping
together, just sleeping together the same dream!
And what if you and I slept the same dream, Rosario?"

"And this woman —— " began the poor girl,
with tears in her voice, trembling within the arms
of Augusto.

"This woman, Rosario, doesn't love me —
doesn't love me — doesn't love me. But she has
shown me that there are other women — and some
woman will be able to love me. Will you love me,
Rosario? Tell me, will you love me?" And he
pressed her madly to his breast.

"I think so — I think I shall love the señorito —— "

"That I shall love you, Rosario, that I shall
love *you*."

"That I shall love you."

"That's the way, Rosario, that's the way, isn't it?"

At that moment the door opened and Liduvina appeared. With an exclamation of "Oh!" she closed it again. Augusto was much more embarrassed than Rosario. Jumping quickly to her feet, she shook herself and smoothed her hair, and in a broken tone she said:

"Well, señorito, shall we attend to the bill?"

"Yes, I had forgotten. But you will come again, won't you? You'll come again?"

"Yes, I'll come again."

"And you forgive me for everything? You forgive me for it?"

"Forgive you — for what?"

"For this, this — it was a fit of madness. You forgive me?"

"I have nothing to forgive you for, señorito. And what you ought to do is not to think about that woman."

"And you — will you think about me?"

"Come, I've got to go."

The bill was settled and Rosario left. She had hardly gone when Liduvina entered the room.

"Weren't you asking me the other day, señorito, how you knew whether a man is in love or not?"

"Yes, I was."

"And I told you that it was by his doing or saying foolish things. Well, then, I can assure you now that you are really in love."

"But with whom? With Rosario?"

"With Rosario? — No, indeed! With the other one."

"And how do you know that, Liduvina?"

"Bah! You have been saying and doing to this girl what you couldn't say or do to the other."

"But do you think —— "

"No, no, of course I don't think that it went too far; but —— "

"Liduvina, Liduvina!"

"Just as you wish, señorito."

The poor fellow went to bed with his head on fire. And as he threw himself into the bed, at the foot of which Orfeo was sleeping, he said to himself, "Ah, Orfeo, Orfeo, this sleeping alone, alone, sleeping a dream alone! The dream of one person alone is an illusion — a mere appearance; the dream of two persons is truth, reality. What is the real world but the dream that we all dream, the common dream?"

And he dropped into a dream.

XIII

ONE morning a few days later Liduvina came into Augusto's room saying that a young lady was asking for him.

"A señorita?"

"Yes, it is she, the piano-teacher."

"Eugenia?"

"Yes, Eugenia. It's clear that you are not the only one who has gone crazy."

Poor Augusto began to tremble. And in fact he felt like a criminal. He rose, washed hastily, dressed, and left his room prepared to face the worst.

"I have learned, Don Augusto," Eugenia said to him solemnly as soon as she saw him, "that you have settled my debt with the creditor, and that the mortgage upon my house is now in your possession."

"I don't deny it."

"And by what right did you do this?"

"By the right, señorita, which any citizen has to buy what he pleases if the owner is willing to sell."

"I am not speaking of that. What I mean is, for what purpose did you buy it?"

"Well, because it pained me to see you dependent upon a man who is probably not interested in you and who, I suspect, is only a pitiless adventurer."

"That is to say, it is your idea to have me dependent upon you — since you really are interested in me —— "

"Oh, nothing of that kind, never, never! Never, Eugenia, never! I am not seeking to make you dependent upon me. You offend me by the very thought of it. You will see." And leaving her alone he went out in a state of extreme agitation.

He returned shortly carrying some papers.

"Here, Eugenia, are the documents that secure your debt. Take them and do what you will with them."

"What do you mean?"

"That I renounce everything. That was the intention that I had in buying them."

"I knew it, and that is just why I tell you that your only aim is to make me dependent upon you. You wish to bind me by gratitude. You want to buy me!"

"Eugenia! Eugenia!"

"Yes, you want to buy me, you want to buy me; you want to buy — not my love, because that can't be bought, but my body!"

"Eugenia! Eugenia!"

"That is the fact, even if you don't think so. It is infamous, and nothing less than infamous!"

"Eugenia, for God's sake, Eugenia!"

"Don't come any nearer, for I don't know what I may do!"

"Then I am surely coming nearer. Hit me, Eugenia, hit me; insult me, spit on me, do anything you wish to me!"

"You don't deserve anything —— " and Eugenia rose. "I am going, but let it be understood that I don't accept your alms, or your gift! I am going to work harder than ever. I'll make my fiancé work — he'll soon be my husband; and we shall be able to live. And as far as this matter is concerned, you may keep my house."

"But really, Eugenia, I am perfectly willing that you marry this fiancé of yours!"

"What do you mean? What do you mean? Tell me plainly!"

"I certainly didn't do this to have you marry me — bound by a tie of gratitude — I really do renounce all happiness for myself! Or rather, it is perfectly true that my happiness consists in your being happy, and in nothing else! And in your being happy with the husband that you freely choose! —— "

"Ah, I see! Now I understand! You are reserving for yourself the rôle of the victim, the rôle of the hero and martyr! Keep the house, I say. I make you a present of it."

"But Eugenia, Eugenia!"

"No more!"

And without looking at him again those two eyes of fire vanished.

For a moment Augusto was beside himself, and he was hardly aware of his existence. When he had shaken off the mist of confusion that enwrapped him he took his hat and rushed out into the street to wander about at random. Coming to the church of San Martín he entered it, hardly knowing where he was. As he entered he could see nothing but the subdued light of the lamp burning in front of the grand altar. All about him seemed to exhale darkness and the odour of age, of tradition perfumed by incense, of the hearth of centuries, and almost groping his way he went over and sat down on a bench. He dropped upon it rather than seated himself. He felt tired, mortally tired, as if all of that darkness and all of that age that he was breathing rested like a weight upon his heart. From out of a murmur that seemed to come from a distance, from a far distance, there emerged now and then a restrained cough. He recalled his mother.

He closed his eyes and dreamed again of that sweet and restful house into which the light en-

tered between the white flowers embroidered upon
the curtains. He saw his mother again, going and
coming noiselessly, always in black, with that smile
of hers that was the sediment of tears. And he re-
lived again all of his life as a son, when he formed
a part of his mother and dwelt under her protec-
tion; and then he thought of the death of the poor
lady, of that gentle, composed, and unhurried
death, without pain, when she departed like a bird
of passage quietly setting out upon its flight. Then
he remembered, or dreamed again, his finding of
Orfeo, and shortly he found himself in a state of
mind in which the strangest pictures passed before
him, as if in a cinematograph.

Close to him a man was whispering his pray-
ers. The man rose to leave and Augusto followed
him. At the door of the church the man dipped the
first and second fingers of his right hand into the
font of holy water and offered holy water to Augusto, afterwards crossing himself. They found
themselves together at the door.

"Don Avito!" exclaimed Augusto.

"It is I, Augustito, it is I."

"But — you here?"

"Yes, I am here. Life teaches us much, and
death teaches more. They teach us more, far more,
than science."

"But what of the candidate for genius?"

Don Avito Carrascal told him the pitiful story of his son.* And he ended by saying: "You see, Augustito, how I have come to this ——"

Augusto remained silent and looked at the ground. They were passing along the Alameda.

"Yes, Augusto, yes," proceeded Don Avito. "Life herself is the only school-mistress of life. There is no pedagogy that will work. One learns to live only by living, and each man has to begin the apprenticeship of life from the beginning ——"

"And what of the cumulative toil of generations, Don Avito, the legacy of the centuries?"

"There are only two legacies, the legacy of illusions and the legacy of disappointments; and the two meet only where we met a short time ago: in the temple. It is certain that you were brought there either by a great illusion or by a great disappointment."

"By both."

"Yes, by both of them, indeed. For illusion, or hope, engenders disappointment, or memory; and disappointment, or memory, will engender in its turn illusion, or hope. Science deals with reality, something present, my dear Augusto, and I am no longer able to live on anything present. Since my poor Apolodoro died, my victim" — and as he said this his voice was choked with sobs — "that is, since

* A story which is told in my *Amor y Pedagogía.*

he killed himself, no present is longer possible for
me; there is neither science nor reality that means
anything. I cannot live except by remembering
him or looking forward to him. And I have gone to
lodge in this home of all illusions and of all disappointments — in the church!"

"And that means that you now believe?"

"How can I say? —— "

"But — you don't believe, then?"

"I don't know whether I believe or do not
believe; I know that I pray. I don't know very well
what my prayer is. There are a certain number of
us who meet here at nightfall to tell the rosary.
I don't know who they are, and they don't know
me, but we feel that we are one and in intimate
communion with one another. And I'll be damned
if I think now that humanity has any need of
geniuses!"

"And your wife, Don Avito?"

"Ah, my wife!" exclaimed Carrascal, and a
tear that showed itself in one of his eyes seemed to
irradiate a light from within. "My wife! I have
discovered her! Up to the time of my tremendous
misfortune I did not know what I had in her. I
penetrated the mystery of life only when, in the
terrible nights following the suicide of my Apolodoro, I rested my head in her lap, in the lap of
the mother, and wept and wept. And she would
say, passing her hand gently over my head, 'My

poor son! My poor son!' Never, never was she more of a mother than then. I never thought in making her a mother (and what for? Only that she might furnish me with the raw material for genius!) — I never thought in making her a mother that I should some day need her as such. For I did not know my mother, Augusto, I never knew her, I never had a mother, I never knew what it was to have one until, when my wife lost her son and mine, she felt herself to be my own mother. You knew your mother, Augusto, the excellent Doña Soledad. Otherwise I should advise you to marry."

"I knew her, Don Avito, but I lost her, and here in the church I was occupied in remembering her."

"But if you wish to have her again, marry, Augusto, marry!"

"No, it wouldn't be she that I should have, I shall not have her again."

"True, but marry!"

"And how?" added Augusto, forcing a smile, and remembering what he had heard of one of the doctrines of Don Avito. "How? Deductively or inductively?"

"No more of those things now! God, Augusto, don't remind me of tragedies! But — after all, if I must fall in with your humour, marry intuitively!"

"And suppose that the woman I love doesn't love me?"

"Marry a woman that loves you, even if you don't love her. It is better to marry to have her win your love than to marry to win hers. Look for one who loves you."

The image of the laundry-girl passed in fleeting view through the mind of Augusto. For he had formed the illusion that the poor child was in love with him.

When finally Augusto took leave of Don Avito he turned in the direction of the Casino. He wanted to clear away the mist in his head, and the mist in his heart, by playing a game of chess with Victor.

XIV

*A*UGUSTO saw that something un-
usual was going on in his friend Victor. Victor was
silent and irritable and lost one game of chess after
another.

"Victor, there's something the matter with
you."

"Yes, old man; yes; there's something serious
the matter. Let's go out; it's a beautiful night; I
will tell you about it."

Although Victor was Augusto's most intimate
friend, he was five or six years older, and he had
been married more than twelve years, having married very young — as a matter of conscience, so
the reports ran.

When they were in the street Victor began:

"You know, Augusto, that I was obliged to
marry when I was very young —— "

"Obliged to marry?"

"Yes, don't make news of it. Everybody has
heard it rumoured. Our parents made us marry,
mine and Elena's, when we were mere children.
And for us marriage was a game. We played at husband and wife. But it turned out to be a false
alarm —— "

"What turned out to be a false alarm?"

"Why, what they married us for. An exaggerated fear of shame on the part of the parents on both sides. They learned of a little slip of ours which caused a bit of scandal, and without waiting to see what the results would be, or whether there would be any, they married us."

"They did well."

"I shouldn't say so. But as it turned out, neither did that slip have any consequences nor any of the slips that followed our marriage."

"Slips?"

"Yes, in our case they were only slips. We went slipping along. I told you that we were playing at husband and wife —— "

"Victor!"

"No, don't be too suspicious. We were too young for any sort of perversion, and we are still too young. But the last thing we thought of was starting a family. We were two young people living together and carrying on what is called the marital life. But a year passes, and then when we see that the marriage is without fruit we begin to put on long faces, to look at each other askance, and to lay the blame on each other. I could not reconcile myself to not being a father. I was now a man, more than twenty-one years old; and frankly, the idea of being inferior to others, inferior to any savage who has his first child punc-

tually nine months after marriage, if not before
— I couldn't resign myself to it."

"But, old fellow, what fault could there
be? —— "

"And of course it goes without saying that I
put the blame upon her; and I said to myself, 'This
woman is sterile, and she is making you ridiculous.'
And I did not doubt that, on her side, she was putting the blame upon me, and even supposed —
well, she may have supposed anything —— "

"But what?"

"Oh, nothing, except that when a year passes,
and another, and another, and there are no children by the marriage, the wife falls into the way
of thinking that it is the husband's fault, and that
it is because he was not sound at the time of marriage, because he had in him some sort of disease —— But the fact is that we felt like enemies
towards each other. The devil had got into the
house. And at last the devil exploded, and it came
to mutual recriminations, and to such things as
'you're no good' and 'you're the one who's no
good' and all the rest of it."

"Could that have been the reason why you
were not well for a while, two or three years after
you were married — so nervous and preoccupied;
when you had to go off alone to a sanitorium?"

"No, that wasn't the reason — it was something worse."

There was a period of silence. Victor gazed at the ground.

"Very well, never mind, keep it to yourself; I don't wish to pry into your private affairs."

"Well, here now, I'll tell you! The fact is that in my exasperation over those domestic quarrels with my wife I came to imagine that it was not a question of intensity, or however you might put it, but of frequency. Do you get my meaning?"

"Yes, I think I do —— "

"And so I plunged into a course of eating like a savage whatever I thought to be especially substantial and nourishing, and everything that was highly seasoned with all kinds of spices, especially with those that are supposed to be aphrodisiacs, and to being with my wife as often as possible. And of course —— "

"You made yourself sick."

"Naturally. And if I had not bethought myself in time and returned to reason, I should have been packing up for another world. But I recovered from that in two senses. I returned to my wife, and we both became calm and resigned. And little by little there came to reign in the house, not merely peace, but even happiness. At the beginning of this new life, when we had been four or five years married, we used to grieve now and then over our solitude; but very soon we were not only consoled, we became habituated to it. And we ended not only by not feeling the want of children, but even by pitying those who had them. We became accustomed each to the other; we inured ourselves each to the practice of the other. You can't understand that —— "

"No, I don't understand it."

"Well, anyhow, I inured myself to the habits of my wife, and Elena to mine. Everything was established upon a basis of regularity in our household; everything, just as the meals were. At twelve sharp, not a minute earlier or later, the soup on the table, and the program is so arranged that we eat every day nearly the same things, in the same order, and in the same quantity. I abhor change, and Elena hates it too. In my house we live by the stroke of the clock."

"Really, this reminds me of what our friend Luis says of the two Romeras: he calls them a bachelor husband and wife."

"And rightly enough, for there is no bachelor who is more of a bachelor or more set in his ways than a married man with no children. It happened once that, to make up for the absence of children — for after all, the paternal instinct had never really died in me, nor the maternal instinct in her — we adopted a dog, or you might say that we made a child of him. But when we saw him one day die before our eyes, because a bone had stuck in his throat, and saw those moist eyes seeming to

appeal to us for life, we were so filled with grief
and horror that we wanted no more dogs or any
other living thing. And we contented ourselves
with dolls, those big stupid-looking things that you
have seen at my house, which my Elena dresses and
undresses again."

"Those won't die on you."

"No, of course not. And so all was going well
and we were most content. No baby's crying dis-
turbs my dreams, nor have I had to worry about
whether it was going to be a boy or a girl, or about
what to do with him or her. And besides, I have
had my wife always comfortably at my disposal, with no interruptions from periods of pregnancy or of lactation; in short, a dream of a
life!"

"Do you know that this differs little, if at all,
from —— "

"From what? From an illicit union? I think so
myself. A married life without children can easily
come to be converted into a kind of legal concu-
binage, very well ordered, very hygienic, relatively
chaste, but after all that's what it is! Husband and
wife both single, but living together as lover and
mistress. And thus eleven years have passed, going
on now to twelve — But now — do you know
what has happened to me?"

"Man, how am I to know?"

"But can't you guess what has happened?"

"Not unless it is that your wife is pregnant —— "

"Just that, my boy, precisely that. Just imagine what a calamity!"

"Calamity? Why, weren't you so eager to —— "

"Yes, at the beginning, during the first two or three years of marriage, not much longer. But now — now the devil has returned to the house, and the quarrels are begun again. And just as in the years past each of us used to blame the other for the sterility of the union, so now each blames the other for this thing that has come upon us. And we are already beginning to call him — no, I won't tell you —— "

"Well, don't tell me if you don't want to."

"We are beginning to call him the intruder! And I have dreamed of his dying on us some morning with a bone stuck in his throat —— "

"Atrocious!"

"Yes, you are right, atrocious. And now farewell to regularity, farewell to comfort, farewell to habits! It was only yesterday that Elena had a fit of vomiting. That seems to be one of the annoyances attached to the state that they call — interesting! Interesting! Interesting! There's something interesting for you — vomiting! Could you imagine anything filthier or more indecent?"

"But isn't she overjoyed at feeling herself a mother?"

"She? As much as I am! This is a vile trick of Providence, of Nature, or whoever it may be; it's a piece of mockery. If it had come — the boy or the girl, whichever it might have been — if he had come when we innocent turtle-doves, filled more with vanity than with paternal love, were looking for him; if he had come when we believed that to be childless was to be inferior to others; if he had come then he would have been a blessing. But now! now! I tell you it is mockery. If it were not for —— "

"What, old man, what?"

"I was going to offer him to you as a companion for Orfeo."

"Man, control yourself and don't talk nonsense —— "

"Nonsense — you are right. Forgive me. But do you think that this is a pleasant thing to have happen to us, at the end of something like twelve years, when things were going so beautifully, and after we had been cured of the silly vanity of the newly married? Truly we were living so tranquilly, so securely, so trustfully —— "

"Man, man!"

"You are right — yes, you're right. But the most awful thing of all is — what do you think?

— that my poor Elena is so obsessed by the sense of being ridiculous and can't rid herself of it. She feels that she has become a laughing-stock."

"Why, I don't see ——"

"No, neither do I see it, but it is so; she feels that she is a laughing-stock. And the things she does make me fear for — the intruder — or the intrudereess."

"Man!" exclaimed Augusto, alarmed.

"No, no, Augusto, no, no! We haven't lost our moral sense, and Elena who, as you know, is deeply religious, respects the intentions of Providence, although she is gnashing her teeth; and she is resigning herself to becoming a mother. And she will be a good mother, I have no doubt of that, a very good mother. But the dread of being ridiculous is so strong in her that to conceal her condition and cover up her pregnancy she is capable of things that — really, I don't want to think about it. Just at present it is a week since she went out of the house. She says that she is ashamed, and that she imagines that everybody on the street will be busy looking at her. And now she is talking of going away somewhere so that, if she is to go out and get the benefit of the sun and the fresh air when her pregnancy is more advanced, she will not be where there are people who know her, and who perhaps may be offering their congratulations."

The two friends were silent for a moment, and after the brief silence had set a seal upon the story, Victor said:

"And so go ahead, Augusto, go ahead and marry, so that something of this kind may perhaps happen to you; go ahead and marry the piano-teacher!"

"And who knows?" said Augusto as if talking to himself. "Who knows? Perhaps if I marry I shall have a mother again —— "

"Mother, yes," added Victor, "mother of your children! If you have children —— "

"And my own mother too! It may be, Victor, that you are now going to find a mother in your wife, a mother for yourself."

"What I shall begin to do now is to lose my nights —— "

"Or to find them, Victor, or to find them."

"After all I really don't know what it is that is happening to me, nor what is happening to both of us. For my own part I think I might come to be resigned; but my Elena, my poor Elena — poor child!"

"There! You see you are beginning to pity her."

"After all, Augusto, think well before you marry!"

And they parted.

Augusto went home with his head full of what he had heard from Don Avito and from Victor. He had now almost forgotten Eugenia and the affair of the cancelled mortgage, and also the laundry-girl.

As he entered the house and Orfeo rushed out with a bound to receive him, Augusto took him up, felt his throat, and pressing him to his bosom, he said: "Be careful about the bones, Orfeo, be very, very careful about them, won't you? I don't want you to choke on one of them; I don't want to see you die before my eyes, appealing to me for life. You know, Orfeo, that Don Avito, the education-ist, has turned back to the religion of his fathers — it's a case of heredity! And Victor can't resign him-self to being a father. Don Avito finds no conso-lation for the loss of his child and Victor finds none for the prospect of having one. But what eyes, Or-feo, what eyes! How they flashed when she said to me, 'You want to buy me! You want to buy — not my love, for that can't be bought, but my body! Keep my house!' I buy her body — her body! My own is already too much for me, Orfeo, my own is too much. What I need is soul. Soul! Soul! And a soul of fire, like that which irradiates from those eyes of Eugenia. Her body — her body — yes, her body is splendid, magnificent, divine; but really her body is soul, pure soul; every part of it

life, meaning, poetry! For myself I have more than
enough body, Orfeo, and I have too much body
because I am wanting in soul. Or may it not be,
rather, that I am wanting in soul because I have
too much body? I touch my body, Orfeo, I take
hold of it, I see it; but my soul — where do I find
my soul? Is it true that I have a soul? I just began
to feel it breathe a little when I was embracing
Rosario; poor Rosarito sitting on my knee; when
she was weeping and I was weeping too. Those
tears couldn't come from my body; they were coming from my soul. The soul is a well-spring that
reveals itself only in tears. Until one sheds real tears
one never knows whether one has a soul or not. And
now let us go to sleep, Orfeo, if, indeed, they let us."

XV

B u t , child, what have you gone and done?" Doña Ermelinda asked her niece.

"What have I done? Just what you would have done in my place if you have any sense of shame, I am sure of it. To think of wanting to buy me! Of wanting to buy *me!*"

"Listen to me, child; it is always better to have somebody wanting to buy you than wanting to sell you. Don't doubt that."

"Wanting to buy me! Wanting to buy *me!*"

"But that isn't so, Eugenia, that isn't so. He has done it out of generosity; it's a case of simple heroism —— "

"I have no use for heroes. That is, for those who are striving to be heroes. When heroism comes of itself, naturally, well and good! But calculated heroism! Wanting to buy me! Wanting to buy *me!* I tell you, Aunt, I am going to make him suffer for this. He's going to suffer for it, this —— "

"This — what? Go on and finish!"

"This — this ill-favoured noodle. I shall treat him as if he did not exist. He doesn't exist anyhow!"

"But what nonsense you keep talking —— !"

"But do you think, Aunt, that this 'uncle' —— ?"

"Who? Uncle Fermín?"

"No, that one — that canary-fellow. Do you think that he has anything inside of him?"

"At least he has his inwards."

"But do you think he has any inwards? Not a bit of it. I tell you, he's hollow — as hollow as if I saw him hollow!"

"But come over here, child, and let us talk quietly. And stop talking and acting foolishly. Forget all of that. I think that you ought to accept him —— "

"But I simply don't love him, Aunt —— "

"You, what do you know about what it means to love? You have had no experience. You may know what a quaver is, or a demisemiquaver, but as for what it means to love —— "

"It seems to me, Aunt, that you are talking for the sake of talking —— "

"But what do you know, child, about what it means to love?"

"But I certainly love somebody else —— "

"Somebody else? Do you mean that loafer, Mauricio, whose soul is so small that it rattles around in his body? Do you call that love? Is he the somebody else? I tell you, Augusto is your salvation, and Augusto only. So cultivated, so rich, so good —— !"

"But that is just why I don't love him, because as you say he is so good. I don't like good men."

"Neither do I, my dear, neither do I, but —— "

"But what?

"They are the men we have to marry. That's what they are born for, and that's what they are good for — for husbands."

"But if I don't love him how am I going to marry him?"

"How? By marrying him, of course! Didn't I marry your uncle?"

"But, Aunt, didn't you —— ?"

"Yes, I think I do now, it seems that I do; but when I married him I doubt if I loved him. Let me tell you, this idea of love is book-stuff, something that has been invented only for the purpose of talking and writing about it. Poetical nonsense! The real thing is matrimony. The civil code doesn't speak of love, and it does speak of matrimony. All this idea of love is nothing but music —— "

"Music?"

"Yes, music. And you know that music is good for hardly anything except to live by teaching it; and that if you don't take advantage of an opportunity like this, it's going to be some time longer before you get out of your purgatory —— "

"What do you mean? Am I asking you for

anything? Am I not earning my own living? Am
I a burden to you?"

"Don't flare up in that fashion, you tinder-
box! And don't say things of that kind or we shall
be quarrelling in earnest. Nobody said anything
to you about that. And everything that I am saying and advising you is for your own good."

"Yes, for my own good — for my own good.
It was for my own good that Señor Don Augusto
Pérez performed that manly action, for my own
good — A manly action, yes, a manly action!
Wanting to buy me! Wanting to buy *me — me!* A
manly action, that's what it is, a manly action —
the kind of thing that men do! Men, I am coming
to see it now, Aunt, men are gross; they are a lot
of pigs. They are entirely without delicacy. They
can't even do you a favour without insulting
you —— "

"All men?"

"Yes, all of them. Those, of course, who are
real men."

"Ah!"

"Yes, because the others, those who are not
gross and piggish and egoistic, they are not men?"

"What are they, then?"

"I don't know what to call them . . . sis-
sies!"

"What theories you have, child!"

"In this house you can't escape the contagion."

"But you have never heard your uncle say anything like this."

"No, it is something that I have thought of myself, from observing men."

"From observing your uncle too?"

"No, my uncle is not a man — not one of that kind."

"Then he is a sissy, is he? A sissy? Come, speak!"

"No, no, no, not that either. My uncle is — well, he's my uncle. I can't get it into my head that he is anything of that other kind — you know what I mean — of flesh and bone."

"Then what do you think that your uncle is?"

"I think that he is only — I don't know how to say it — he's just my uncle. You see, it's as if he somehow didn't really exist?"

"That may be your idea of it, child, but I can tell you that your uncle does exist. You can bet that he exists."

"Pigs, pigs, pigs, all of them. Do you know, Aunt, what that barbarian Martín Rubio said to poor Don Emeterio a few days after Don Emeterio had lost his wife?"

"No, I think I haven't heard it."

"Well, the story is this. It was at the time of the epidemic — you remember. Everybody was very terrified, and during part of the day you didn't let me go out of the house, and I was drinking boiled water. Everybody was avoiding everybody else, and if you saw anyone newly in mourning, it was as if he were pest-ridden. Well then; five or six days after losing his wife poor Don Emeterio had to leave his house — he was in mourning, of course — and he ran into that barbarian Martín. When Martín saw that Don Emeterio was in mourning he kept at a certain prudent distance from him as if he feared contagion, and he said to him, 'But, old fellow, what is the matter? Has anything happened in your family?' 'Yes,' replied poor Don Emeterio, 'I have just lost my wife —— ' 'How unfortunate! And how — how did it happen?' 'She died in childbirth,' Don Emeterio told him. 'Ah, that's not so bad,' replied the barbarian Martín, and then he stepped up to shake hands. Have you ever heard of anything more manly and more chivalrous? A manly act! I tell you, they are a lot of pigs, nothing but pigs."

"It's better that they should be a lot of pigs than a lot of vagabonds, like that dunce Mauricio, for example, who has got your head full of him, I don't understand how. For according to what I hear, and I can assure you that it is well grounded, I'll be blest if this idiot is really in love with you —— "

"But I am in love with him, Aunt, and that is enough."

"And do you think that that fellow — your lover, I mean — is really a man? If he were really a man he would have got started long ago and found some work."

"Well, if he is not a man, I want to make him one. It is true that he has the fault you mention, Aunt, but perhaps that is why I love him. And anyhow, since that manly act of Don Augusto — wanting to buy me, to buy *me!* — since then I am resolved to stake everything on one throw and marry Mauricio."

"And what are you going to live on, you unhappy child?"

"On what I earn! I shall work, and work more than I do now. I shall accept lessons that I have hitherto rejected. In any case, I have given up that house; I have presented it to Don Augusto. After all, it was a whim, only a whim. It was the house I was born in. And now, relieved of the bother of the house and relieved of the mortgage on it, I shall set to work more energetically. And Mauricio, seeing me work for both of us, can't then avoid looking for work and working himself. That is, if he has any sense of shame —— "

"And if he hasn't?"

"Well, if he hasn't — then he will be dependent upon me!"

"Yes, he'll be the piano-teacher's husband!"

"Let it be so. He will be mine, mine! And the more dependent, the more mine."

"Yes, yours — as a dog might be yours. That is what is called buying a man."

"Hasn't a man with his money wanted to buy me? Then what is there strange about it that I, a woman, with my work, should want to buy a man?"

"All this that you are saying, child, sounds very much like what your uncle calls feminism."

"I don't know anything about that, and I don't care to know. But I can tell you, Aunt, that the man who can buy me has not yet been born. Buy *me — me!*"

At this point in the conversation the servant entered to say that Don Augusto was waiting to speak to the señora.

"He? Oh, go away from here! I don't want to see him. Tell him that I have said all that I have to say."

"Think it over, child, think it over quietly; don't take it in this fashion. You haven't understood what Don Augusto really meant."

When Augusto found himself in the presence of Doña Ermelinda he began by asking her to accept his explanations. He was deeply pained, he said; Eugenia had not understood his real intentions. For his part, he had formally cancelled the mortgage upon the house, which was now legally released from any such burden and at the disposal of its owner and mistress. She might persist in refusing to receive the rents but he would not be able to collect them himself; so that the money would be lost without profit to anyone; or rather it would go on being deposited to credit of the owner. Moreover, he renounced his pretensions to the hand of Eugenia and he desired only that she might be happy; he was even ready to look for a good situation for Mauricio, so that he would not have to live on his wife's income.

"You have a heart of gold!" cried Doña Ermelinda.

"All that is needed now, señora, is that you should convince your niece of the real nature of my intentions, and that she should forgive me if this cancellation of the mortgage was an impertinence. But it seems to me that there is no use now of thinking about the past. If she wishes, I will be her sponsor at the wedding. And then I shall set out for a long and distant journey."

Doña Ermelinda called the maid and told her to call Eugenia and tell her that Don Augusto wished to speak to her. "The señorita has just gone out," was the maid's reply.

XVI

Y o u are impossible, Mauricio," Eugenia was saying to her lover in the doorman's box, "utterly impossible; and if you go on in this way, if you don't bestir yourself and shake off this torpor, if you don't do something to find a position, so that we can marry, I am capable of doing something startling."

"Startling? How startling? Come, tell me, sweetheart" — his hand was caressing the girl's neck while he curled a lock of her hair around one of his fingers.

"I want to tell you something: if you like we can marry just as it is, and I will go on working — for both of us."

"But what will people say of me, woman, if I agree to anything of that kind?"

"What difference does it make to me what they say about you?"

"Well, well, this sounds serious."

"Yes, what they say about you doesn't interest me. What I want is to put an end to this as soon as possible ——— "

"Is it as bad with us as all that?"

"Yes, it is bad, very bad. And if you don't make up your mind quickly I am capable of —— "

"Of what, then?"

"Of accepting the sacrifice of Don Augusto."

"Of marrying him?"

"No, never that! Of taking back my property."

"Well, do it, then, sweetheart, do it! If this is the solution, and there is no other —— "

"And you have the nerve —— "

"It doesn't call for nerve! This poor Don Augusto strikes me as not quite right in his head, and since he has this whim I think we ought not to thwart him —— "

"Which means that you —— "

"Why, of course, sweetheart, of course!"

"A man, after all a man!"

"Not so much of a man as you might wish, judging from what you say. But come here —— "

"Come, Mauricio, let go of me. I have told you a hundred times that you are not to be —— "

"That I am not to be affectionate —— "

"No, that you are not to be — gross! Be quiet. And if you want any more favours from me you will have to shake off this laziness and look for work in earnest, and — you know the rest. And so, let's see if you are sensible, eh? Remember that I gave you a box on the ear the last time."

"And how good it felt! Go ahead, sweetheart,

and give me another! See, here's my face —— "
"Don't say very much about it or —— "
"Go ahead, then!"
"No, I don't want to give you that pleasure."
"Or any other?"
"I've told you not to be gross. And I tell you again that if you don't hurry and find work, I am capable of accepting that offer."
"Very well, then, Eugenia, do you want me to speak to you with my heart in my hand — the truth and the whole truth?"
"Speak!"
"I love you immensely, really I do. I'm completely gone on you. But this business of marrying scares me and fills me with a horrible fear. I am temperamentally a loafer, I have to admit it; I was born that way. What troubles me most is to be obliged to work. And I foresee that if we marry, and since I suppose you will want us to have children —— "
"Well, that's the limit!"
"I am going to be obliged to work; and since living is expensive I shall have to work steadily. And as for allowing you to be the one to work, never! Never! Mauricio Blanco Clará can't live by a woman's work. But there may be a solution which will provide for everything without my having to work or you either —— "

"Let's have it ——"

"But — will you promise, child, not to be angry?"

"Go on and tell me!"

"From everything that I have heard, it seems that this poor devil of a Don Augusto is a noodle, a ——"

"Go ahead and say what you were going to say!"

"But you mustn't be offended."

"I've told you to go on!"

"Well, as I was going to say, he is — predestined to be made use of. And perhaps the best thing would be, not merely to accept this offer of the house, but ——'"

"But what?"

"To accept him as a husband."

"Indeed?" — and she rose to her feet.

"You accept him and then, since he is a poor fool of a man — everything is arranged ——"

"Everything is arranged? What do you mean by that?"

"Yes, he does the paying, and we ——"

"We — what?"

"Well, we ——"

"Not another word!"

Eugenia went out with her eyes flashing fire. "But what beasts! What beasts! I never should have believed it — What beasts!" And going home she locked herself in her room and burst into tears. Later she developed a fever and had to go to bed.

For a moment or two Mauricio seemed somewhat taken aback. But he very soon recovered his self-possession and, lighting a cigarette, he walked down the street, whispering something pretty to the first comely girl that passed close to him. That evening he happened to be talking to a friend about Don Juan Tenorio.

"That guy is not very convincing to me," Mauricio was saying. "You don't find that kind of thing anywhere off the stage."

"And is it you who say that, Mauricio, you who have a reputation as a Tenorio and a seducer?"

"Seducer? I a seducer? What stories they invent, Rogelio?"

"But what about the piano-teacher?"

"Bah! Do you want me to tell you the truth, Rogelio?"

"Out with it!"

"Well then, of every hundred affairs, more or less chaste — and you understand that the one you were referring to is perfectly chaste — of every hundred affairs between a man and a woman, in more than ninety she is the seducer and he is the seduced."

"What do you mean? Are you going to deny

that you have made a conquest of Eugenia, the piano-teacher?"

"Yes, I do deny it. It is not I who have made conquest of her, but she who has made a conquest of me."

"Seducer!"

"Say what you please, the seducer is she. I couldn't resist her."

"For the case in hand that makes no difference —— "

"But I think that the affair is about to end, and that I am going to find myself free again. Free from her, of course; for I can't guarantee that no other woman will make a conquest of me. I am so weak, you know! If I had been born a woman —— "

"Yes, but why is the affair going to end?"

"Because — well, I have put my foot into it! I wanted our relations to go on, or rather I wanted them to begin — you understand — without obligations or consequences. But really it looks now as if she is going to give me the mitten. This woman wanted to take possession of me completely."

"And she will end by doing so!"

"Who can tell? I am so weak! I was born to be supported by a woman, but with dignity and self-respect, you understand — otherwise not."

"And what do you understand by dignity and self-respect? Might one ask?"

"Man, that is the kind of question one doesn't ask. There are some things that can't be defined."

"Very true!" replied Rogelio in a tone of deep conviction, adding: "But if the piano-teacher drops you what are you going to do?"

"Why, remain disengaged for a while and see whether someone else makes a conquest of me. I have been conquered so many times, you know! — But this girl, with her trick of never yielding, of keeping herself always at a respectable distance, of remaining chaste, in short — for in that matter nobody could be stricter — with all this she's had me absolutely daffy over her, absolutely daffy! She might have ended by doing anything she pleased with me. And now, if she drops me I shall feel it, and rather badly, but I shall be free."

"Free?"

"Free, yes, for another woman."

"It is my opinion you'll be making it up with her —— "

"Who can tell? But I doubt it. She has a bit of a temper — And today I seem to have insulted her; yes, I certainly did insult her."

XVII

*A*UGUSTO,'' said Victor to him, "do you remember Don Eloíno Rodríguez de Alburquerque y Alvarez de Castro."

"Do you mean that clerk in the Treasury who was so fond of going on a spree, and preferred a spree on cheap liquor?"

"The same. Well — he got married."

"A fine old carcass for the woman who loads herself up with him."

"But the astonishing thing is the way he came to be married. Listen, and take note! You know that Don Eloíno Rodríguez de Alburquerque y Alvarez de Castro, in spite of all his surnames, had hardly enough even to die on, really nothing but his salary in the Treasury. And besides, he was completely broken in health."

"The life he had lived."

"Well, the poor devil was suffering from an affection of the heart, from which he could not recover. His days were numbered. He had just pulled out of a very tight squeeze which had set him down at death's door — and which then brought him to matrimony; but another — and it was all up with

him. The situation was this. The poor fellow was
going from one boarding-house to another and having to leave every one of them, because for four
pesetas a day you can't expect many delicacies or
fancy-dishes, and he was very exacting. And he
wasn't overly clean. And so, wandering about from
house to house, he landed finally in one kept by a
venerable landlady, a person well on in years and
older than himself — and you know he was nearer
sixty than fifty — and twice a widow. The first
husband was a carpenter who committed suicide
by throwing himself off a scaffold into the street,
to whom she often refers as *her* Rogelio. The second was a sergeant of the carabineers who left her
a little sum at his death, yielding her a peseta a day.

"And now, behold! Don Eloíno, upon finding
himself in the house of this widow-lady, takes it
into his head to fall ill, seriously ill, so ill indeed that
it looked as if he were past hope and dying. First
they called in Don José to see him, and afterwards
Don Valentín. But the man seemed bent upon dying! And his illness called for so much nursing, and
of such a sort, at times not altogether pleasant,
that it consumed all of the landlady's time, and the
other boarders began threatening to leave. And
here was Don Eloíno, who could afford to pay very
little more, and the twice-widowed lady telling
him that she couldn't keep him in the house any
longer because it was injuring her business.

" 'But for Lord's sake, señora, for charity's sake!' he seems to have said to her. 'Where can I go in this condition? In what other house are they going to take me? If you put me out, I shall have to go off and die in a hospital. For Lord's sake, for charity's sake! For the few days that I have to live! —— ' For he was convinced that he was dying and would die very soon. But for her part she told him — and reasonably enough, since her house was not a hospital — that she got her living out of her business and that the business was now being injured.

"Just at this time one of Don Eloíno's fellow clerks at the office conceived a saving idea. He said to him:

" 'There is one way, Don Eloíno, and only one way, by which this good lady can be recompensed for keeping you in her house while you live.'

" 'What is that?' asked Don Eloíno.

" 'First,' said the friend, 'I want to know what you yourself think about your illness.'

" 'Ah, what I think is that I have only a short time to live, a very short time. It may be that my brother and sister will not reach here in time to see me alive.'

" 'Do you think it is as bad as that?'

" 'I feel that I am dying —— '

" 'Well, if that is the case, there is a way of

keeping this good lady from firing you out into the street and compelling you to go to a hospital.'

" 'And what is it?'

" 'By marrying her.'

" 'Marry *her*? Marry the landlady? Who, I? A Rodríguez de Alburquerque y Alvarez de Castro! Man, I am in no condition for joking!' And it seems that the incident produced such an effect upon him that he nearly died upon the spot."

"What you might expect."

"As for the friend, as soon as he recovered from his first shock of surprise, he made it clear to Don Eloíno that by marrying the landlady he was leaving her a widow's pension of thirteen *duros* a month, of which no one would get the benefit otherwise, and it would go to the state. You see, then —— "

"Yes, friend Victor, I know of more than one man who has married only to prevent the state from saving his pension. That is what you call civic virtue!"

"But if Don Eloíno rejected the proposal with indignation, just imagine what the landlady had to say:

" 'I? Marry at my years? And for the third time? And this old carcass? Ugh, disgusting!' However, she consulted the physician, and being assured that Don Eloíno had only a few days to live, she ended by accepting the proposal, remarking that, 'Thirteen *duros* a month would suit me very well.' Then she called in the parson, the good Don Matías, a saintly man as you know, to finish the work of persuading the dying man.

" 'To be sure, to be sure I will,' said Don Matías. 'Poor fellow! Poor fellow!' And he succeeded.

"Then Don Eloíno sent for Correíta, with whom he had quarrelled, and told him, they say, that he wished to be reconciled with him, and asked him to be a witness at the wedding. 'What! Are you going to be married, Don Eloíno?'

" 'Yes, Correíta, I am marrying the landlady, Doña Sinfo! I, a Rodríguez de Alburquerque y Alvarez de Castro, just think of it! I am marrying her in return for nursing me for the few days of life that remain to me — I doubt whether my brother and sister will arrive in time to see me alive — and she marries me for the pension of thirteen *duros* a month that I leave her.' And the story goes that when Correíta went home and told his wife Emilia, as he naturally would, she exclaimed,

" 'But, Pepe, you were stupid! Why didn't you tell him to marry Encarna? For the thirteen *duros* a month she would have nursed him just as well as that old woman.' (Encarnación is the servant, neither young nor pretty, whom Emilia brought with her to the household as a kind of dowry.) And it is reported that Encarna added, 'Quite right,

señorita. I could just as well have married him, and
for the thirteen *duros* I would have nursed him for
the time he has to live, which won't be long.' "

"I believe that you are inventing all this, Victor."

"Well, I'm not. There are some things that
can't be invented. And the best is yet to come. Don
Valentín, the physician who attended Don Eloíno
after Don José, told me that upon one of his visits,
finding Don Matías there in his vestments, he
thought he had come to administer Extreme Unc-
tion; and then he was told that they were marrying
him. And when he returned a little later, the land-
lady-bride (for the third time!) accompanied him
to the door and asked him in an anxious and rueful
tone,

" 'But tell me, Don Valentín, is he going to
live? Will he still go on living?'

" 'No, señora, no; it is a question of
days ——— '

" 'He'll die soon, then, won't he?'

" 'Yes, very soon.'

" 'But you are sure he'll die?' "

"Atrocious!"

"And this isn't all. Don Valentín ordered that
they should give the patient nothing but milk, and
only a little at a time; but Doña Sinfo said to another boarder:

" 'No, indeed! I am going to give him everything that he asks for! Why cut off his pleasures if he has such a short time to live! —— ' But when she was ordered to give him an enema, she said, 'I give him an enema! Ugh, how disgusting! This old carcass! No, I won't, I won't! If he were one of the other two, those I loved, those that I married because I wanted to! But this one! No! —— ' "

"This is all utterly fantastic!"

"No, it is historic. The brother and sister of Don Eloíno arrived then; and prostrated by the disgrace of it, the brother said,

" 'To think of my brother, my brother, a Rodríguez de Alburquerque y Alvarez de Castro, marrying the keeper of a boarding-house in the Calle de Pellejeros! My brother, the son of a former President of the Audiencia of Zaragoza, of Za-ra-go-za, marrying a — Doña Sinfo!' He was utterly overcome.

"But the suicide's widow, the bride of the dying man, said to herself: 'And now we'll see, it's as plain as day: because I am their sister-in-law they will go off without paying me their board, although I have to live by it!' But it seems that they did pay their board, and the husband paid his board too, but they took away a gold-headed cane that belonged to him."

"And did he die?"

"Yes, but some time afterwards. He got better, considerably better. And the landlady said, 'Don Valentín is to blame for this; he must have understood the illness. It would have been better to have Don José, who didn't understand it. If Don José alone had attended him, he would be dead by this time and off my hands.'

"Doña Sinfo, besides the children of her first husband, had a daughter by the second, the carabineer, and shortly after the marriage Don Eloíno said to the daughter, 'Come here! Come here and let me kiss you, for I am now your father and you are my daughter.'

" 'Not your daughter,' said the mother, 'only your adopted daughter!'

" 'Step-daughter, you mean, señora, step-daughter! Come here — I am bequeathing you —— '

"And the story is that the mother grumbled: 'The shameless rascal said that only to coax her into familiarities with him! — Did you ever see the like of it! —— '

"And presently, of course, came the rupture. 'That was a swindle, Don Eloíno, a pure swindle. For if I married you it was only because they assured me that you were dying and would die very shortly; and if you weren't going to die — then I was fooled! They deceived me, Don Eloíno, they deceived me.'

" 'They deceived me too, señora. But what is it you would like me to have done? Die for the sake of pleasing you?'

" 'That was the understanding.'

" 'Never mind, señora, I shall be dying soon enough — and sooner than I should wish —— '

"Then they quarrelled over a matter of a few *cuartos* more or less in the price of board, and she wound up by putting him out of the house.

" 'Good-bye Don Eloíno, may you fare well!'

" 'May God be with you, Doña Sinfo!'

"And at last he died, the third husband of this lady, leaving her a pension of 2.15 pesetas a day, besides five hundred pesetas which were given her for mourning. Of course she didn't spend it for mourning. The most that she did was to have a couple of masses said for him, partly out of remorse, and partly out of gratitude for the pension of thirteen *duros*."

"My God, but what a story!"

"But not an invented story. It would not be possible to invent such a story. I am engaged just now in collecting the facts about this tragicomedy, this funereal farce. I thought at first of making a one-act play of it. But thinking it over again I have decided to incorporate it somehow — in the same way that Cervantes inserted the shorter stories in his *Don Quixote* — in a novel that I am writing to divert my mind from the worry and anxiety that my wife's pregnancy is causing me."

"But do you mean that you have set yourself to write a novel?"

"What else should I be doing?"

"And what is the plot of it, may I ask?"

"My novel hasn't any plot; or rather, the plot is what comes out of it. It makes its own plot."

"What do you mean?"

"Well, it's this way. One day when I didn't know what to do, but felt a very deep longing — an inner urge, a tickling of the imagination — to do something, I said to myself: I am going to write a novel, but I am going to write it, just as we live, not knowing beforehand what is coming. I sat down, took some paper, and began with the first thing that occurred to me, without knowing what would follow, without any plan whatever. Each of my personages will develop just as he happens to act and speak, especially as he happens to speak; his character will go on being formed step by step. At times his character will consist in not having any."

"Yes, like mine."

"I don't know. That remains to be seen. I merely allow myself to be carried along."

"And is there any psychology in it? Any descriptive passages?"

"What there is in it is dialogue; and dialogue

above everything else. It is a matter of having the characters talk, and talk a good deal, even if they say nothing."

"Elena must have suggested that to you, didn't she?"

"Why?"

"Because once when she asked me for a novel, to kill time with, I remember that she told me she wanted it to have a good deal of dialogue, and in sentences short and crisp."

"Yes, whenever she finds in a novel long descriptions, or discourses, or narratives, she snaps out, 'Padding! Padding! Padding!' For her the only part that isn't padding is the dialogue. And you know, of course, you can just as well distribute a sermon through a dialogue —— "

"But why should you have to do so?"

"Because people like conversation for the sake of conversation, even when it says nothing. There are those who can't stand a speech of half an hour and yet will spend three hours chattering in a café. It's the charm of conversation, of talking for the sake of talking, of talking in a fashion broken and interrupted."

"I must confess that I also find the steady rhythm of a speech rather wearing —— "

"Yes, it's the gratification that men find in talk, in living talk — And especially in having it seem that the author himself is not speaking and annoying us with his personality, his satanic ego. And yet of course all that my characters say, I am saying —— "

"That is true up to a certain point —— "

"To a certain point? What do you mean?"

"Yes, you may begin by thinking that you are guiding them, with your own hand, but you may easily end in the conviction that it is they who are guiding you. It often happens that an author ends by being the plaything of his own inventions —— "

"Perhaps. But in any case I expect to put into this novel everything that happens to occur to me, whatever it may be."

"Then it will end by not being a novel."

"No, it will be — it will be — a *nivola*."

"*Nivola*? What in the world is that?"

"Well, I once heard the poet, Manuel Machado, the brother of Antonio, tell the story of how he took a sonnet to Eduardo Benot, to read it to him. The sonnet was written in Alexandrians or in some other heterodox form of verse. He read it to him, and Don Eduardo said: 'But this is not a sonnet! —— '

" 'No, señor,' replied Machado, 'it is not a sonnet, it is — a *sonite*.'

"Well, it's the same with my novel. It is not going to be a *novel*, but — what did I say? — *navilo — nebulo —* no, no, *nivola*; that's what it is, a *nivola*! For then none will have the right to say that I am annulling the laws of their *genre* —— I am making up the *genre* (and to make up a *genre* is only give it a new name), and I am giving to it the laws that please me. And plenty of dialogue!"

"But when the character is alone, then what?"

"Then — a monologue. And in order that it shall have some of the appearance of a dialogue, I bring in a dog, to whom the character addresses himself."

"Do you know, Victor, I have an impression that you are inventing me —— "

"Perhaps I am!"

After they had separated Augusto walked along talking to himself as usual. "This life of mine? Is it a novel? Or a *nivola*? Or what is it? All of this that is happening to me, and happening to the others about me, is it reality or is it fiction? May not all of it perhaps be a dream of God, or of whomever it may be, which will vanish as soon as He wakes? And therefore when we pray to Him, and cause canticles and hymns to rise to Him, is it not that we may lull Him to sleep, rocking the cradle of His dreams? Is not the whole liturgy, of all religions, only a way perhaps of soothing God in his dreams, so that He shall not wake and cease to dream us? Ah, my Eugenia! my Eugenia! And my Rosarito —— "

"Hullo, Orfeo!"

Orfeo, who had run out to meet him, was frisking about and trying to climb up his legs. He picked him up and the little animal began to lick his hand.

"Señorito," Liduvina said to him, "here is Rosarito with the washing waiting for you."

"Why didn't you settle with her and let her go?"

"Well, I didn't know — I told her that the señorito couldn't be very long in coming, and that if she wanted to wait —— "

"But you could have settled with her yourself as you have done before —— "

"Yes, but — you understand me —— "

"Liduvina! Liduvina!"

"It is better for you to settle with her yourself."

"I'll go and see her."

XVIII

"*H*ULLO, Rosarito," cried Augusto as he entered the room.

"Good evening, Don Augusto." The girl's voice was calm and serene and her countenance was not less calm and serene.

"Why didn't you settle with Liduvina, as you have always done before when I was not at home?"

"I don't know! She told me to wait. I thought there might be something you wanted to say to me —— "

"But — is this simplicity? Or what is it?" thought Augusto, and he paused, wondering what he should say. There was a moment of embarrassment filled with uneasy silence.

"What I want you to do, Rosario, is to forget what happened the other day. I don't want you to think of it again. Do you understand me?"

"Very well, just as you wish —— "

"Yes, that was a piece of folly — folly. I hardly knew what I was doing or what I was saying — just as I don't know now either —— " And he began drawing near to the girl.

She awaited him tranquilly and with an air of

resignation. Augusto seated himself on the sofa and called her: "Come here!" He told her to sit on his knee as she had done before, and then for some time he gazed into her eyes. She stood his gaze quite calmly, but her whole body trembled like an aspenleaf.

"You're trembling, child —— ?"

"I? Not I? It seems to be you —— "

"You mustn't tremble. Be still —— "

"Don't make me cry again —— "

"Ah, yes, really you want me to make you cry again. Tell me, have you a lover?"

"But what a question —— "

"But tell me, have you?"

"A lover — well, not a regular lover — no!"

"But hasn't any young fellow of your own age ever shown you any attention?"

"But you see, Don Augusto —— "

"And what did you say to him?"

"There are some things that you don't talk about —— "

"Of course. But come, tell me, do you love one another?"

"My Lord, Don Augusto! —— "

"Listen, if you are going to cry I shall leave you."

The girl bent over and hid her head on Augusto's chest, and in the effort to keep herself from sobbing she burst into tears. "This child is going to faint on me," thought Augusto as he stroked her hair.

"Come, calm down! Calm yourself!"

"And that other woman? —— " asked Rosarito without raising her head, as she choked down her sobs.

"Ah, you haven't forgotten her? Well, the other woman has ended by sending me off for good. I had never really won her, but now I have lost her — lost her for good and all!"

The girl raised her head and looked him steadily in the eyes, as if to see if he were speaking the truth.

"You want to fool me —— " she whispered.

"Why should I want to fool you? Ah, yes, I see, I see now! And so that's what's the matter, is it? But didn't you say that you had a lover?"

"I didn't say anything at all —— "

"Quiet! Quiet!" And placing her beside him on the sofa he rose and began to pace the floor.

But as he turned his gaze in her direction he saw that the poor girl had changed colour and was trembling. And then he perceived that he had left her without support; and that, seated alone on the sofa, and facing him at a distance, like a criminal before a magistrate, she felt on the verge of fainting.

"True!" he cried. "We seem to be safer the nearer we are together."

He sat down again, put her again on his knee, encircled her with his arms, and pressed her to his breast. The poor child put one arm over his shoulder, as if for support, and again hid her face in his bosom. But when she heard there the hammering of his heart she became alarmed.

"Are you feeling ill, Don Augusto?"

"And who can ever say that he is well?"

"Don't you want me to call and have them bring you something?"

"No, no, let it go. I know what my complaint is. And what I need is to take a trip." And after a moment of silence: "Will you go with me?"

"Don Augusto!"

"Drop the 'Don'! Will you go with me?"

"Just as you wish ———"

A mist invaded the mind of Augusto. The blood began to throb in his temples and he had a feeling of oppression in his chest. Seeking relief, he began to kiss Rosario on her eyes, so that she had to close them. Suddenly he rose, and freeing himself from her he said:

"Leave me! Leave me! I am afraid!"

"Afraid? Afraid of what?"

The unexpected serenity of the maiden frightened him still more.

"I am afraid, I don't know of whom; of you, of myself, of anybody you please! Of Liduvina! Listen to me, go away now, go away! But you'll come again, won't you? You'll come again?"

"Whenever you wish."

"And you'll go with me on my journey. You'll do that, won't you?"

"Just as you direct —— "

"But go away now, go!"

"And that other woman —— "

Augusto rushed up to the girl, who had now risen to her feet, caught hold of her, pressed her to his breast, joined his own dry lips to her lips, and held her there for a moment without kissing her, his mouth pressed to hers, shaking her head from side to side. Presently he released her: "Go along, be off!"

Rosario left the room. She had hardly gone when Augusto, as thoroughly exhausted as if he had just returned from a tramp of leagues in the mountains, threw himself upon his bed, put out his light, and dropped into a monologue:

"I have been lying to her, and I have been lying to myself as well. It's always that way. Everything that I say is make-believe, and there is nothing that is not make-believe. Whenever a man talks he lies, and so far as he talks to himself — that is to say, so far as he thinks, knowing that he thinks — he lies to himself. The only truth in human life is that which is physiological. Speech — this thing that they call a social product — was made for lying. I have heard one of our philosophers say that truth is also a social product, like speech; truth is what all persons believe, and, by all believing the same thing, they understand one another. A social product? That which is a social product is never truth, but lie —— "

Feeling a tongue licking his hand, he called out: "Ah, you here, Orfeo? Well, you don't lie because you don't talk. And I almost believe that you never go wrong — you don't lie to yourself. And yet, being the domestic animal that you are, some of the human traits must have stuck to you. We men do nothing but lie and make ourselves important. Speech was invented for the purpose of magnifying all of our sensations and impressions — perhaps so that we could believe in them. Speech along with the other conventional forms of expression such as kissing and embracing. None of us does anything but play his part in a play. We are all just so many characters, so many masks, so many comedians! No one either suffers or enjoys what he means by his words — and perhaps believes that he suffers or enjoys. If he did, he would never be able to live. At bottom we are so utterly quiescent — just like myself lying here, playing my little comedy all alone, actor and spectator both at once! The only pain that kills is physical pain. The only genuine man is the physiological man, the man who doesn't speak, hence the man who doesn't lie —— "

He heard a knock at the door.

"What is it?"

"Aren't you going to eat supper tonight?" asked Liduvina.

"That's so! Wait a moment and I'll be there.

"And when night comes I shall sleep, as I sleep other nights; and she will sleep too. But will Rosarito sleep? Shall I not have disturbed the tranquillity of her spirit? And that natural manner of hers, is it innocence or is it cunning? But perhaps there is nothing more cunning than innocence; or rather, nothing more innocent than cunning. Yes, yes, I have always thought that there is nothing more — more — how shall I put it? — nothing more cynical than innocence. Yes, that calmness with which she yielded herself to me, that calmness that filled me with fear, fear of I really don't know what — that was nothing but innocence. And her saying, 'And that woman?' Jealousy, eh? Jealousy? It is probable that love is never born without jealousy being born too; it is jealousy that brings the revelation of love. Let a woman be ever so much in love with a man, or a man with a woman, they are not conscious that they are in love, they don't even tell themselves that they are in love, that is to say, they don't really fall in love, until he sees that she is looking upon another man or she sees that he is looking upon another woman. If there were only one man in the world and one woman, and no further society, it would be impossible for them to fall in love with one another. In any case there is always need of a go-between, the Celestina; and society is the great Go-Between. *El Gran Galeoto!* The Great Go-Between! How well that comes in! Yes, *El Gran Galeoto!* Were it only for the sound of the words. And therefore all this business of love is only one lie more. And the physiological side of it? Bah, this physiological affair is not love or anything like it! And for this reason it is truth! But — come, Orfeo, let us go and get supper. That is certainly truth!"

XIX

T w o days later Augusto was told that a lady was waiting to speak to him. He left his room to receive her and found Doña Ermelinda. To the astonished "You here?" of Augusto she replied by saying, "Since you would not call upon us again —— "

"You understand, señora," replied Augusto, "that after what happened to me in your house the last two visits that I made there — once when I saw Eugenia alone, and the other time when she was unwilling to see me — it was not possible for me to call again. I stand by what I have said and done, but I can't call again —— "

"Well, then, I have come here as the bearer of a commission to you, sent by Eugenia."

"By Eugenia?"

"Yes, by her. I don't know what has happened to her in the affair with her lover, but she is furious with him and won't have him mentioned. And the other day when she returned home she shut herself in her room and refused to take any supper. Her eyes were red from weeping, but from the tears that scald, you understand, tears of rage —— "

"Ah, but are there different classes of tears?"

"Of course. There are tears that relieve and refresh, and tears that only suffocate and burn the more. And she kept repeating that refrain of hers, that all of you men are beasts, and nothing but beasts. And for several days past she has been going about with a long face and as cross as if she had seven devils in her. That is, until yesterday. Yesterday she came to me and told me that she was sorry for all that she had said to you, that she had gone too far and had been unjust to you. She recognizes now the rectitude and the nobility of your intentions, and she wishes you, not indeed to forgive her, for saying that you wanted to buy her, but to know that she doesn't believe anything of the sort. She makes a special point of this. She says that above everything she wishes you to believe that, if she did say that, it was because she was feeling angry and spiteful, but she doesn't really believe it —— "

"I don't think that she believes it."

"And after that — after that she commissioned me to find out from you diplomatically —— "

"And the best diplomacy, señora, is not to practice any, especially with me —— "

"After that she asked me to find out whether it would displease you if she accepted the gift that you had made her of her own house, but without committing herself —— "

"Without committing herself? What do you mean?"

"Why, of course that she is to accept the gift simply as a gift."

"But if I offer it simply as a gift, what right has she to accept it as anything else?"

"Well, she says that she is willing to accept it. As a proof of her good will and of the sincerity of her regret for what she said, she is prepared to accept your generous present, only it must not imply —— "

"Stop, señora, stop! I fear that unwittingly you are about to insult me again —— "

"But I had no intention —— "

"It is said that the worst insults are at times those that are inflicted without intention."

"But I don't understand —— "

"And yet the point is a very simple one. I was once at a social gathering where there was a man present who knew me and did not even greet me. As I was leaving I complained of this to a friend, and he said:

" 'Don't be surprised. He hasn't done it deliberately. He hasn't even noted your presence.'

"And I answered: 'But that is just what makes it ruder: not that he didn't salute me, but that he neglected even to note my presence.'

" 'He has done so unintentionally; it is a case of absent-mindedness —— ' he replied.

"And I rejoined: 'The greatest rudenesses are those that are called unintentional, and the greatest rudeness of all is to be absent-minded in the presence of other persons.' It is the same kind of thing, señora, as that which is very stupidly called unintentional forgetfulness. As if it were ever possible to forget a thing intentionally! Unintentional forgetfulness is generally simple rudeness."

"And pray what is all this leading to?"

"To this, Señora Doña Ermelinda: that after she has begged my pardon for the offence of saying that I was trying to buy her with my gift, and thus to force her gratitude, I don't very well see what she means by accepting it and at the same time stipulating that she is not to be committed. Committed to what, indeed, committed to what?"

"Please don't get so excited, Don Augusto! ——"

"I am not to get excited, señora! Do you think that I am going to let this — this girl make sport of me? Does she think that she can play a game with me?" As he said this he happened to be reminded of Rosarito.

"Goodness gracious, Don Augusto, goodness gracious!"

"I have already said once for all that I cancelled the mortgage and that the mortgage has been vacated, and that if she fails to take charge of her house, at any rate I have nothing to do with it. And whether she thanks me or not, makes no difference to me whatever!"

"But, Don Augusto, please don't get so stirred up about it. Really, all that she wishes is to make her peace with you and to be friends again! —— "

"Yes, now that she is at war with the other one, isn't that it? Before this I was the other one; now I am the one, am I not? And now it is a matter of angling for me, isn't it?"

"But surely I have said nothing like that! —— "

"No, but I have grasped your meaning."

"Then you have deceived yourself completely. For immediately after my niece had said what I have just repeated to you, when I attempted to insinuate the advice that, having quarrelled with that loafer of a lover, she should now try to win you as such — you understand me, of course —— "

"Yes, that she should reconquer me —— "

"Exactly! Well then, when I gave her this advice, she said to me a hundred and one times, no, and no, and no! She esteemed you and valued you as a friend, but she did not care to have you for a husband; and she did not wish to marry any man unless she were in love with him —— "

"And that she could never be in love with me, didn't she say that?"

"No, she didn't quite say that."

"Come, now, señora, this is more diplomacy —— "

"What do you mean?"

"Why this! You have come here not merely to ask that I forgive this — this girl, but to see whether I will not agree to become again a suitor for her hand, isn't that true? It's an understood thing, isn't it? And in the end she agrees to become resigned —— "

"I swear to you, Don Augusto, I swear to you by the sacred memory of my mother — may she be in glory! — that —— "

"Remember the second commandment: don't swear —— !"

"Very well, then, I swear this to you: it is you who are now forgetting yourself, and you are forgetting — unintentionally, of course — who I am. You forget that you are speaking to Ermelinda Ruiz y Ruiz."

"And if it were as you said —— "

"It is so, I assure you." And she uttered these words with an emphasis that left no room for question.

"Well, in that case — in that case — you may say to your niece that I accept her explanation, and that I am deeply grateful, that I shall continue to be her friend, a loyal and noble friend, but only a friend, you understand, nothing but a friend. And then you need not tell her that I am not a piano upon which she can play anything that occurs to her; that I am not the kind of man that she can drop today and take up tomorrow; that I am not a substitute, or a vice-sweetheart; that I am not a place at the second table —— "

"But don't get so excited!"

"I assure you, I am not at all excited! Tell her, then, that I will continue to be her friend —— "

"And you will come to see us soon?"

"As for that —— "

"Remember that if you don't the poor child will not believe me, and she's going to feel hurt —— "

"The fact is, I am thinking of setting out upon a long and distant journey —— "

"But you will come before you leave, to say good-bye —— "

"Very well, we'll see —— "

They separated. When Doña Ermelinda arrived home and repeated to her niece the conversation with Augusto, Eugenia said to herself: "There's another woman in the case! No question about that! Now I shall certainly go after him and catch him again."

As for Augusto, as soon as he was alone he started in to walk up and down the room, all the while saying to himself: "She wants to play upon

me as if I were a piano — she drops me, takes me
up, and then she'll drop me again — I was being
held in reserve. Say what she will, she is aiming to
get me at her feet again, perhaps to revenge herself — or possibly to make the other man jealous
and twist him around her fingers. As if I were a
puppet, a guy, a Don Nobody. But I have a character of my own, you bet I have! I am I! Yes, I
am I! I am I! To be sure, I owe it to Eugenia — I
can't deny that — that the amorous instinct has
been awakened in me; but having once awakened
and aroused it, she is no longer needed by me. What
we have in superfluity is women."

At this point he could not help smiling. For he
was reminded of a remark of Victor's when Ger-
vasio, just recently married, informed them that
he was going with his wife to spend a short time in
Paris. "To Paris and with a woman? That is like
taking along codfish to Scotland!" This had amused
Augusto immensely.

And he continued his soliloquy: "What we
have in superfluity is women. And how charming
the cunning innocence, or the innocent cunning,
of Rosarito, this new edition of the eternal Eve!
What a delight of a girl! Eugenia brought me down
from the abstract to the concrete, but Rosarito has
brought me to the generic. And there are so many
attractive women in the world, so many — so many
Eugenias, so many Rosaritos! No, no; nobody can

play a game with me, and least of all a woman. I am
I! My soul may be small, but it is mine!" And feeling, somehow, in this exalted state of his ego, as if
his ego were swelling and swelling, and the house
becoming too contracted for it, he went out into
the street to give it relief and breathing-space.

Once he had put his foot into the street, and
found the clear sky over his head, and the people
coming and going, each occupied with his own
business or pleasure, and no one paying attention to
Augusto (unintentionally, of course), or bothering his head about him (doubtless because no one
knew him) — then he felt his ego, the ego of "I
am I," beginning to grow smaller and smaller, fold-
ing up within his body, and seeking even there a
tiny nook in which to lie curled up and out of sight.
The street was a cinematograph; and he felt that he
too was becoming something cinematographic —
a shadow, a phantasm. It happened always that a
bath in the human multitude, losing himself in the
mass of men coming and going without knowing
him or taking note of him, gave him the same effect
as a bath out in the open country, under the open
sky with the breezes blowing about him.

When he was alone and by himself he was always aware of himself. Alone, he could say (though
he might say it only to convince himself), "I am
I"; in the presence of the rest of men, mixed with

the multitude of the busy or the idle, he ceased to be aware of himself.

And so he arrived at the modest little garden forming part of the solitary plaza of the retired quarter in which he lived. This plaza was a quiet piece of backwater where there were always children playing, because no tram-cars passed here and very few carriages; and a number of elderly men enjoying the sun in the short and mild autumn afternoons, when the leaves of the dozen Indian chestnuts growing here in seclusion, after trembling before the north wind, were strewn about the walks or covered the seats of the wooden benches — all of these painted green, the colour of the leaves when fresh. Those domestic, urban trees, planted strictly in order, regularly irrigated, when it was not raining, by a system of ditches, and spreading their roots beneath the flags of the walk — those captive trees which waited to see the sun show itself above the roofs of the houses and then set behind them — those caged trees, homesick perhaps for the distant forest, had a mysterious attraction for Augusto. In their branches the birds were singing, likewise urban; of the kind that learn to be wary of the children, but now and then draw near to the old men who offer them crumbs of bread.

How many times, seated solitary and alone upon one of the green benches of that little square, he had gazed upon the fire of the setting sun above the roof of a house, and now and then upon a black cat on the top of a chimney, standing out against the brilliant golden glow of the clouds! And meanwhile, in the autumn, it was raining yellow leaves — broad leaves like those of a vine, but now like so many hands mummified and pressed into thin sheets — upon the little gardens in the centre, with their borders and pots of flowers. And the children went on playing among the dry leaves, playing perhaps at gathering them together, taking no notice of the fiery sunset.

When he arrived today at this tranquil spot and seated himself on a bench, not without first brushing off the leaves — for it was autumn — some small boys were playing, as usual, nearby. And one of them, pushing another up against the trunk of one of the Indian chestnuts, said to him,

"You were prisoner here, some robbers had you —— "

"But I —— " began the other peevishly; and the first replied,

"Yes, but you were not you; you were a prisoner." Augusto wanted to hear no more; he rose and went to another bench. And he said to himself,

"We grown-ups play the same game. You are not you! I am not I! And these poor trees — are they they? Their leaves fall earlier, much earlier than those of their brothers in the mountains, and

they turn into mere skeletons; and with their backs
to the brilliant rays of the electric light, these skeletons then project their silhouetted shadows upon
the walks. A tree illuminated by an electric light!
What a strange, what a fantastic appearance is
given by its foliage in the early spring when the
arc-light gives it that metallic sheen! And here
too where they are not tossed by the breezes!
Poor trees, that may not enjoy one of those black
nights in the country, one of those nights without
a moon, under a mantle of palpitating stars! It
seems that man, in planting these trees here, must
have said to each of them, 'You are not you.' And
lest they forget, he has given them this nocturnal
illumination by electric light — lest they sleep. Poor
sleepless trees! Poor night-watchers! No, no, they
can't play with me the game they are playing with
you."

He rose and began to walk the streets, up and
down, like a somnambulist.

XX

SHOULD he set out on the journey
— yes or no? He had now announced it; first, to
Rosarito, just for the sake of saying something, and
without knowing what he was saying — or rather,
as a pretext for asking whether she would go with
him; and then to Doña Ermelinda, in order to
prove to her — what? What was he aiming to prove
by telling her that he was about to set out on a
journey? Well, whatever it may have been, the
fact was that he had twice committed himself. He
had said that he was about to undertake a long and
distant journey and he was a man of character —
he was himself, Augusto. Must he now show, then,
that he was a man of his word?

A man of his word is a man who says a thing
first and thinks about it afterwards; and then,
whatever may be the result of thinking about it,
he does what he said. Men of their word never cor-
rect a mistake, never go back on what they have
said. And he had said that he was about to undertake a long and distant journey.

A long and distant journey! Why? What for?
How? And whither?

The servant announced that a young lady was waiting to see him.

"A young lady?"

"Yes," said Liduvina, "I think it must be — the piano-teacher!"

"Eugenia?"

"The same."

For a moment he was astounded and unable to reply. During an instant of irritation the idea flashed across his mind of sending her off again — of having them say that he was not at home. "She comes here to make a conquest of me, to play with me as if I were a doll," he said to himself. "She wants to amuse herself with me as a substitute for the other fellow." Presently he thought better of it. "No, I must show her that I am resolute."

"Tell her that I am coming at once."

He was thrilled with the idea of the woman's boldness. "It must be admitted that she is a real woman, every inch a personality. What nerve! What resolution! And what eyes! But no, no, no! She doesn't bend me! She can't win me!"

When Augusto entered the drawing-room, Eugenia was standing. He motioned to her to take a seat; but she exclaimed before doing so, "They have deceived you, Don Augusto, just as they have deceived me" — the result being that the poor man at once felt himself disarmed and without a word

to say. They both sat down and a moment of silence followed.

"Yes, Don Augusto, it is just as I have said.
They have deceived you with regard to me, and
they have deceived me with regard to you. That
is the whole story."

"But surely we have talked to each other, Eugenia!"

"Don't pay any attention to what I said to
you. The past is past!"

"Yes, the past is always past. It can't very well
be anything else."

"But you understand me. And what I now
wish is that you shall not attribute to my accept-
ance of your generous gift any other meaning than
what it has."

"Just as I wish, señorita, that you shall not
attribute to my gift any other meaning than what
it has."

"Just so. Loyalty for loyalty; each of us ex-
pects the other to be true to himself. And so, since
we must talk frankly, it is my duty to tell you that,
after all that has passed, and after what I said to
you, I could not, even if I wished, think of repaying
you for this generous gift otherwise than by the
purest gratitude. Just as, on your part, I believe —— "

"You are right, señorita. After what has
passed, and after what you said to me in our last

interview, after what the señora, your aunt, said
to me, and after what I surmise, I could not, on my
part, even though I desired to do so, think of putting a price on my generosity ——— ”

"We are in agreement, then?"

"In perfect agreement, señorita."

"And so, will it be possible for us again to be
friends, good friends, true friends?"

"It will."

She extended to Augusto her finely shaped
hand, white and cold as the snow, with tapering
fingers made for ruling the keys of the piano, and
he clasped it in his own, which just then was trembling.

"We shall be good friends, then, Don Augusto.
However, for me this friendship will mean ——— ”

"Will mean what?"

"In the eyes of people generally perhaps ——— ”

"What? Speak! Speak!"

"But you know that there are certain things
which, after some recent painful experiences, I
have now renounced ——— ”

"Explain yourself more clearly, señorita.
There is no use of saying things by halves."

"Very well, then, Don Augusto, let us put the
matter clearly, quite clearly. Do you suppose that,
after what has passed, it is now likely that anyone
who knows, as all of our acquaintances do know,

that you have lifted the mortgage on my patrimony, thus making me a present of it — is it likely that anyone will now approach me with certain intentions in mind?"

"This woman is diabolical!" thought Augusto; and he lowered his head and gazed at the floor, not knowing what to say in reply. When he looked up a moment later he saw that Eugenia was wiping away a furtive tear.

"Eugenia!" he exclaimed; and his voice trembled.

"Augusto!" she whispered weakly.

"But what are we to do? What is it that you wish?"

"Oh, nothing, nothing. It is ill fortune, nothing but ill fortune. We are the playthings of fate. It is simply adversity!"

Augusto was rising from his armchair and moving toward the sofa to take a seat by the side of Eugenia.

"Listen, Eugenia! For God's sake, don't play with me! Ill fortune! The ill fortune is you. There's no ill fortune in this matter but you. It is you who send me hither and thither and spin me round as if I were a top; it is you who drive me crazy; it is you who make me break my firmest resolutions; it is you who bring it about that I am no longer I — "

He put his arm around her neck, drew her towards him, and pressed her to his breast. She quietly removed her hat.

"Yes, Augusto, it is an ill fate that has brought us to this. Neither—neither you nor I can be untrue or disloyal to ourselves. You can't let it seem that you want to buy me, as I put it to you once in a moment of confusion, nor can I seem to be making a substitute of you, a second choice, a place at the second table, as you once said to my aunt, interested only in rewarding your generosity —— "

"But what matters the seeming to us, Eugenia dear, whether it be one thing or another? In whose eyes would it seem so?"

"In our own!"

"But why, Eugenia dear? —— "

He pressed her to himself again and covered her eyes and her forehead with kisses. Both of them were breathing audibly.

"Let me go! Let me go!" she said as she straightened herself up and smoothed her hair.

"No, you—you—you—Eugenia—you—— "

"No, I cannot — it cannot be —— "

"Do you mean that you don't love me?"

"As for loving — who knows what it is to love? How do I know? I don't know — I can't be sure of it —— "

"Then, what about this — just now?"

"This — this is a misfortune of the moment!

The effect of repentance — I don't know what — things of this kind have to be put to the test. And besides had we not agreed, Augusto, that we were to be friends, good friends, but nothing more than friends?"

"Yes, but —— What was it you said about your sacrifice? What about the fact that because you had accepted my gift, and because you are a friend of mine, though only a friend, no one will think of marrying you?"

"Oh, that makes no difference now; my mind is made up!"

"Perhaps after breaking off with —— "

"Perhaps —— "

"Eugenia! Eugenia!"

Just then a knock was heard at the door, and Augusto, tremulous, his cheeks inflamed, called out with a dry voice, "What is it?"

"Rosario. She is waiting for you!" replied Liduvina's voice.

Augusto changed colour and became perfectly white.

"Ah!" exclaimed Eugenia, "I seem to be disturbing you. It is — Rosario who is waiting for you. Don't you see that we cannot be more than friends, good friends, very good friends?"

"But Eugenia —— "

"Rosario is waiting for you —— "

"When you rejected me, Eugenia, as you did

reject me, telling me that I wanted to buy you, and that in any case you loved another, what was I to do after learning to love by meeting you?"

"Come, Augusto, let me have your hand; we shall see one another again, but it is understood that the past is past."

"No, no! The past — past? No! No! No!"

"Come, come, Rosario is waiting ——"

"For God's sake, Eugenia ——"

"After all there's really nothing strange about it. For me too there used to be someone waiting — Mauricio. We shall see one another again. And let us be sincere and loyal to ourselves."

She put on her hat, gave her hand to Augusto — who grasped it, raised it to his lips, and covered it with kisses — and then left the room, accompanied by him to the door. He watched her as she descended the stairs, gallantly and with a firm step. From the landing below she looked up and greeted him with her eyes and waved her hand.

Augusto turned back, entered the sitting-room, and seeing Rosario standing there with her basket of clothes, he said to her brusquely, "What is the matter?"

"Don Augusto, I believe this woman is deceiving you ——"

"And how does that concern you?"

"Everything about you concerns me."

"What you mean is that I am deceiving you —— "

"That is just what does not concern me."

"Are you going to make me believe, girl, that after the hopes I have led you to conceive, you are not jealous?"

"If you knew, Don Augusto, how I have been brought up, and the family I come from, you would understand that although I am a girl, I am placed where I cannot be jealous?"

"Be quiet!"

"Just as you please. But I tell you again that this woman is deceiving you. If it weren't so, and if you loved her, and she were your choice, what could I want more than to have you marry her?"

"Really now, in all this that you are saying are you telling me the truth?"

"I am telling you the truth."

"How old are you?"

"Nineteen."

"Come here!" — and grasping her by the shoulders with both hands, he held her facing him, and stood looking into her eyes.

It was Augusto, however, who changed colour, and not she.

"The truth is, child, I don't understand you."

"I know you don't."

"I don't know what it all means, whether it is

innocence, or cunning, or mockery, or precocious-
ness and perversity —— "

"It is only affection."

"Affection? Why should you feel affection for
me?"

"Do you want to know why? You won't be
offended if I tell you? You promise not to be offended?"

"Go on and tell me."

"Well, then, it is because — because — because you are a poor unhappy man —— "

"And this from you too?"

"Say what you please. But put your trust in
this child, put your trust in — Rosario. More faithful to you — well, not even Orfeo! —— "

"Forever?"

"Forever!"

"Come what may?"

"Yes, come what may."

"You — you are the true —— " and he attempted to catch hold of her.

"No, not now. When you are calmer. And
when you have not just —— "

"That's enough. I understand."

They parted.

After he was alone Augusto kept saying to
himself: "Between one and the other of them they
are going to drive me stark mad — I am not now
myself, I am not I —— "

While Liduvina was serving his dinner she said to him, "I think that the señorito ought to go in for politics or something of the sort; something that would serve as a distraction."

"Why, woman alive, what made you think of that?"

"Because it is better to find distraction for yourself than to have others distracting you and — well, you can see for yourself!"

"Very good, then call your husband Domingo when I have finished eating, and tell him that I want to play a game of ombre with him — to distract myself."

As they were playing the game Augusto suddenly dropped his cards on the table and asked:

"Tell me, Domingo, when a man is in love with two women at the same time what had he better do?"

"It all depends!"

"It all depends — how?"

"Yes, if he has plenty of money, and can stand it, he can marry them both. If not, he shouldn't marry either of them."

"But, man, that first thing isn't possible!"

"Everything is possible if a man has plenty of money!"

"But suppose they find out?"

"It won't make any difference to them."

"Why, man, do you think it is going to make
no difference to a woman to have another woman
taking away part of her husband's affection?"

"She'll be content with her own share, señorito, if he doesn't put a limit on the money she is
to spend. What irritates a woman is to have her
husband limiting her food and dress and everything
else of that kind, cutting off her luxuries. But if he
lets her spend what she wants —— And yet if
she has children by him——"

"If she has children, what then?"

"This is where the real jealousy comes from,
señorito, from the children. It is not one wife that
can't put up with another wife, but one mother
that can't put up with another mother, or with one
who is going to be a mother. It's the mother that
can't stand having her children slighted for the
sake of other children, or for the sake of another
woman. But if she has no children, and he doesn't
put a limit on the table, or the wardrobe, or the
display, or the swagger, bah! he's even relieving her
of some annoyance. If a man has a woman who
costs him money, and then another who doesn't
cost him anything, the one that costs him much
isn't likely to be jealous of the one that costs nothing. And besides costing nothing, she also brings
in money — if he brings to one woman the money
that he gets from another, then ——"

"Then?"

"Then he has all that his mouth asks for. Believe me, señorito, there are no female Othellos —— "

"Nor male Desdemonas."

"Perhaps not! —— "

"But what surprising stuff you are giving me —— "

"Well you see, señorito, before I married Liduvina and came to be a servant in the señorito's household, I served in quite a number of grand houses — and I cut my teeth in them —— "

"But what of your own class?"

"My own class! Bah! there are certain luxuries that we don't indulge in —— "

"And what do you call luxuries?"

"Oh, those thing that you see in the theatres and read about in novels —— "

"Why, man, do you suppose that of the crimes that are called crimes of passion, crimes due to jealousy, only a few are found in your class? —— "

"Bah! that is because these — these rascals go to the theatre and read novels. If they didn't —— "

"And if they didn't —what?"

"Everybody likes to play a part of some kind, señorito, and nobody is the person that he is to himself, but only the person that the other people make him."

"You are a philosopher —— "

"Yes, that is what the last master I had used to call me. But I think, señorito, that my Liduvina has the right idea, and you ought to go in for politics."

XXI

Y es, you are right," Don Antonio was saying to Augusto one afternoon when they were alone together in a quiet corner of the Casino. "You are right, there is a painful, a very painful secret in my life. Doubtless you have suspected something. You have been only a few times at my home — my home; can I call it home? — but you must have noted something —— "

"Yes, something unusual, a kind of sadness in the air, that awakened my sympathy."

"In spite of my children, my poor children! it must have seemed to you a home without children, perhaps even a home without husband and wife —— "

"I can hardly say what —— "

"We came from a distance, from a long distance, with the idea of getting away from —— But there are some things that stay always with one, surrounding and enveloping one like a kind of fateful circle. My poor wife —— "

"Yes, in your wife's face one can read a whole life of —— "

"Of martyrdom — you might as well say it.

Very well, then, friend Don Augusto, it happens
that among our acquaintances you are the one who
— I am not sure why, perhaps because of a certain
underlying affinity — has shown the greatest regard for us, and perhaps the most commiseration.
And so, to comfort myself once more with the idea
that I am relieving my mind of a burden, I am going to confide to you the story of my misfortunes.
This woman, the mother of my children, is not
my wife."

"That is what I supposed. And yet if she is
the mother of your children, and lives with you as
your wife, then she really is your wife."

"No, I have another wife — a legitimate wife,
as they say. I am married, but not to the woman
you have met. And this woman, the mother of my
children, is married too, but not to me."

"Ah! a double —— "

"No, a quadruple affair, as you will see. I married, madly in love — yes, madly in love with her
— a reserved and silent little woman who spoke
little but seemed always to mean much more than
she said; with soft, strangely soft, blue eyes that
seemed to sleep and only to wake now and then,
but then woke to flash fire. And she was all just
like that. Her heart, her whole soul, her body —
they seemed most of the time to sleep. Then suddenly they awoke as if with a shock of surprise;
but only shortly to fall asleep again, the flash of

life having passed. And oh what a life! And then
it was as if nothing had ever been, as if she had
forgotten all that had happened. It was as if we
were always beginning life afresh, as if I were
constantly setting out to win her again. She engaged herself to me in something like an epileptic
attack, and I believe that it was in another attack
that she gave herself to me before the altar. I never
could get her to say to me whether she loved me or
not. As often as I asked her, both before and after
our marriage, always did she reply: 'This is fool-
ishness; one doesn't ask such questions.' At other
times she used to say that the verb 'to love' is
really not used outside of books or off the stage;
and that if I had ever said to her in a letter, 'I love
you!' she would have dismissed me at once. In this
strange fashion we lived through two years of married life, with me making each day a fresh attempt
to win that sphynx. We had no children. One day
she failed to return home in the evening. I was like
a madman; I went everywhere searching for her.
On the following day I learned from a letter, which
was very curt and brief, that she had gone far off,
very far away, with another man —— "

"And had you suspected nothing? Hadn't you
anticipated —— ?"

"Nothing! My wife was accustomed to go out
alone quite often, to her mother's house, or to the
houses of friends; but the peculiar coldness of her

disposition saved her from any suspicion on my
part. And so I had never known what was going
on inside of that sphynx! The man that she fled
with was a married man; and he had not only for-
saken a wife and a little daughter to go off with
my wife, but he had carried with him all of his
wife's fortune, having got it completely into his
own hands. That is to say, not only did he abandon
his wife, but he robbed her and ruined her. And
in that letter, curt and brief and cold, that I received from my wife, allusion was made to the
situation in which the other poor wife was left
by the abductor of mine — abductor or abducted,
I hardly know which! For some days I neither
slept nor ate nor took any rest. I did nothing but
walk the streets of the most distant wards of the
city in which I lived. And I was on the verge of
plunging into the lowest and vilest forms of dis-
sipation. But when my grief began to subside and
to be converted into thought, I remembered the
other poor victim, the wife who had been left destitute, robbed both of her affection and of her fortune. And it seemed to me that, since my wife
had been the cause of her misfortune, it was a matter of duty for me to go to her and offer her pecuniary assistance — in view of the fact that God
had given me a fortune."

"I can guess the rest, Don Antonio."

"Never mind, let me continue. I went to see

her. Imagine what our first meeting was like. We wept over our respective misfortunes, which amounted to a common misfortune. I said to myself, 'And so it was my wife, was it not, for whom he deserted this woman?' And I felt a certain inward satisfaction — why shouldn't I tell you the truth? — something rather unintelligible perhaps, as if it had meant that I had known how to choose better than he, and he had then recognized the fact. And she — his wife — experienced a similar reflection, as she explained to me afterwards, though with the terms reversed. I offered her pecuniary assistance, any part of my fortune that she might need, and at first she rejected the offer. 'I shall work to support my daughter and myself,' she said. But I insisted, and insisted so strongly, that she ended by accepting. Then I proposed that she should come and live with me and be my housekeeper — making it clear, of course, that we should live far away from our home — and after thinking it over for some time she accepted that too."

"And of course in coming to live together —— "

"No, that was later, some time later. That was the after-effect of our having lived together, and the effect also of a certain community of vengeance, of spite, and of I don't know what. Indeed I was not so much taken with her as I was with the child, the unfortunate daughter of my

wife's lover. For her I conceived the love of a
father, an intense paternal love, such as I have for
her today; for I love her as much, yes, perhaps more
than I love my own children. I used to take her
in my arms, press her to my bosom, cover her with
kisses, and then weep, and weep, over her. And the
poor child would say, 'Why are you weeping,
Papa?' For I had her taught to call me 'Papa' and
to regard me as her father. And then the poor
mother, seeing me weep, wept also, and at times
our tears were mingled over the little blond head
of the daughter of my wife's lover, of the daughter of the thief of my happiness.

"One day," he continued, "I learned that my
wife had had a child by her lover, and that day
everything within me rose in rebellion. I suffered as
I had never suffered before, and I thought I should
go mad and kill myself. I had never known the
meaning of jealousy, of the vulgar and brutal sort
of jealousy, until then. The wound in my soul,
which had seemed healed, broke open afresh and
bled. And it bled fire! I had lived more than two
years with my wife, with my own wife, and nothing had come of it! And now this thief! I formed
the idea that my wife had now awakened once for
all and that she was living at a white heat. The
other woman, the one who was living with me,
heard something of the matter and she asked me,
'What is wrong with you?'

" 'Leave me alone,' I replied. But I ended by confessing it all to her, and as she heard me she trembled. And I think that with the contagion of my own jealousy I also infected her —— "

"And of course, after that —— "

"No, it came about some time later, and along quite another path. It happened that one day when we were both in the same room with the child, and I had the little girl on my knee, and was telling her stories, and kissing her, and talking nonsense to her, the mother approached and began to caress the child too. And then she, the poor little darling! put one of her little hands on my shoulder and the other on her mother's, and she said, 'Daddy — Mommy — why don't you bring me a little brother to play with me, like the other children have, so that I shan't be alone?' We both turned white. We looked one another in the eye with those glances that lay bare the soul. We saw our souls stripped bare. And then, to hide our embarrassment, we began loading the child with kisses; and one of the kisses missed its mark. That night, amidst tears and the madness of jealousy, we engendered the first little brother of the daughter of the thief of my happiness."

"A strange story!"

"But our love, if you wish to call it that, was an arid and silent love, made up of rage and fire and no tenderness of speech. My wife — I mean

the mother of my children, because she is my wife
and no one else — my wife, as you must have seen,
is a well-favoured person, and perhaps even beautiful; but she never inspired me with the fire of
desire, and that in spite of our living together.
And even after it had ended in what I have just
told you, I did not conceive myself to be very
deeply in love with her — until something happened to convince me of the contrary.

"It happened once, after one of her confine-
ments — after the birth of our fourth child, in fact
— she was so ill, so desperately ill, that I thought
she was dying. She had lost most of the blood in
her veins, and she lay there white as a wax figure,
with her eyes closed. I thought that I was losing
her. I went very nearly mad. I too was as white as
wax, and the blood was freezing in my veins. I
went to a remote corner of the house, where no
one would see me, and there I fell on my knees and
prayed that God would kill me rather than permit
that sainted woman to die. I wept, and tore at my
flesh, and scratched myself to the point of drawing blood. And then I saw how strong was the tie
that bound my heart to the heart of the mother of
my children. When she had recovered consciousness and was somewhat better and out of danger,
I put my mouth to her ear as she lay in bed, smiling with the renewal of life, and I said to her
what I had never said to her before and never had

wished to say to her as I said it then. And while I was speaking she lay there smiling, smiling, smiling with her eyes fixed upon the ceiling. Then I put my lips to her lips and brought her bare arms around my neck, and I ended by weeping with my eyes directly over hers. She said to me, 'Thank you, Antonio, thank you; for myself, for our children, for all of our children — for each of them — and for her too, for Rita.' Rita is our eldest daughter, the daughter of the thief — no, no, *our* daughter, *my* daughter. The thief's daughter is the other one, the daughter of the woman who once called herself my wife. And now do you understand it all?"

"Yes, and I understand much more. Don Antonio."

"Much more?"

"Yes. Really, you have two wives, Don Antonio."

"No, no, I have only one; only one, the mother of my children. The other is not my wife. I don't know whether she is even the wife of the father of her daughter."

"But this atmosphere of sadness —— "

"The law is always sad, Don Augusto. And the saddest of all loves is that which is born and nurtured over the grave of another, like a plant nourished by the decay of another plant. The crimes — yes, it was the crimes of others that brought us together; and may it be that our union too is a crime? Yet they broke what ought never to have been broken; why, then, was it not for us to join the broken ends?"

"And you have never heard anything more of them —— "

"We wanted to hear no more. Our Rita is now nearly a young lady, and some fine day she will be getting married. But under my name, you understand, under my name; and then let the law do what it will. She is not the daughter of the thief, but my daughter; it is I who have brought her up."

XXII

WELL, then, tell me all about it,"
said Augusto to Victor. "What kind of a reception
did you give to the intruder?"

"Ah, I never should have believed it. Never!
Up to the very eve of his birth our irritation was
still at its height. And even while he was fighting
for entrance to the world, you cannot imagine the
insults that Elena kept hurling at me. 'You, you are
to blame. You!' she repeated. And again, 'Go away
from here! Get out of my sight! Aren't you
ashamed to be sitting here? If I die it will be your
fault.' And at other times, 'This once and never
again, never again!' But he was born and everything is changed. It is as if we had just awakened
from a dream and had just been married. As for
me, I have gone blind, utterly blind; blinded by
this little one. I am so blind that although everyone is telling me that Elena, as the result of her
child-bearing, presents a most forlorn appearance,
that she has dwindled to a skeleton and aged at least
ten years, yet to me she has never seemed so luxuriantly fresh and youthful nor, for the matter of
that, so round and plump."

"This reminds me, Victor, of the story of the rocket-maker that I heard in Portugal."

"Let's have it."

"You know that in Portugal this thing that they call pyrotechnics, or fireworks, amounts to a veritable art. One who hasn't seen fireworks in Portugal doesn't know all that can be done with them. And the nomenclature that they have invented! My goodness!"

"But let's have the story."

"I am coming to it. In one of the Portuguese villages there was a designer of fireworks, or rockets, who had a most beautiful wife, his pride, his consolation, and his delight. He was madly in love with her, but his pride was even greater than his love. He took a peculiar delight in setting the teeth on edge, so to speak, of the rest of mortal men, and he went up and down the world beside her with the air of saying to other men: 'Do you see this woman? Does she appeal to you? She does, does she? Well, she is mine, and mine alone! Now put that in your pipe and smoke it!'

"He was never weary of enlarging upon the beauty and excellence of his wife, and he even claimed that it was she who was the inspiration of his most beautiful pyrotechnic productions, the muse of his fireworks. But now it happens that on one occasion when he is getting ready for an exhibition, with his beautiful wife standing by his side as usual to be his inspiration, the powder catches fire, an explosion takes place, and both husband and wife have to be carried away unconscious, both of them terribly burned. The wife was burned over a large part of her face and breast, in such a fashion that she was horribly disfigured. But the rocket-maker himself had the good fortune to be completely blinded, so that he never saw the disfigurement of his wife. And so it happened that after the accident he was still as proud of her as ever; he continued to enlarge upon her beauty to everyone that he met; and he went on walking by her side — now being led by her — with the same air and manner of challenging arrogance as before. 'Have you ever seen a more beautiful woman than my wife?' he would ask. And everybody, knowing his story, took pity on the poor rocket-maker and praised the beauty of his wife."

"And what of it? Wasn't she still beautiful for him?"

"Perhaps even more beautiful than before, as your wife is for you since she presented you with the intruder."

"Don't call him that!"

"But it was your own name for him."

"Yes, but I don't want to hear it from anybody else."

"It often happens that way. A nickname that you have applied to somebody yourself sounds very different when you hear it used by someone else."

"Yes, they say that no one knows his own voice —— "

"Or his own face. I can tell you at least this about myself: one of the things that fill me most with fear is to stand before a mirror, looking at my face in the glass, alone, when no one sees me. I end by being doubtful of my own existence. And then, seeing myself as somebody else, I come to imagine that I am a dream, an entity of fiction —— "

"Then don't look at yourself in that fashion —— "

"I can't help it. I have a mania for introspection."

"Then you will end like the fakirs, who are said to be absorbed in the contemplation of their own navel."

"And it seems to me that if no one knows his own voice or his own face, neither does he know anything else that belongs to him — that is, anything that is so much his own as to be part of himself —— "

"His wife, for example."

"Precisely. It strikes me that it must be impossible to know the woman who shares one's life and who in the end forms a part of oneself. Have you ever heard what was said by one of the greatest of our poets, Campoamor?"

"No, what?"

"Well, he said that when a man marries, assuming that he marries because he has really fallen in love, at first he cannot touch his wife's body without a violent attack of carnal desire. But the time passes, he grows accustomed to her, and the day comes when it is the same thing to touch the bared thigh of his wife as to touch his own. But then it is also true that if one of her limbs had to be amputated, it would pain him the same as if it were his own."

"Yes, and that is really the case. You don't know how I suffered at the time of the birth!"

"She suffered more."

"Who can tell? And the truth is, it is just because she is something of mine and part of me that I have taken so little account of their saying that she has become ugly and deformed — just as a man takes no account of the fact that he himself is becoming deformed in growing old and ugly."

"But do you think that a man really doesn't note the fact that he is growing old and ugly?"

"Yes, and in spite of all his assertions to the contrary. That is, if the process is steady and gradual. Of course if anything happens to a man to bring about a sudden change —— But as for feeling yourself grow old, not a bit of it! What you feel is that the things around you are growing old, or growing young. And that is the only thing about which I feel regretful now in having a child. For you know what parents point to their children and say: 'Look at them! They are the ones who make us old!' I think that to see a child growing up is both the sweetest thing in the world and the most terrible. Don't marry, then, Augusto! If you wish to enjoy the illusion of eternal youth, don't marry."

"And what am I going to do if I don't marry? How am I going to pass the time?"

"Devote yourself to philosophy."

"But isn't it likely that matrimony is the best, and possibly the only school of philosophy?"

"No, man, no. Have you never noted how many philosophers have been bachelors? And how many great philosophers? Leaving out those who were monks, just think of Descartes, of Pascal, of Spinoza, of Kant —— "

"Don't talk to me about bachelor philosophers!"

"And what about Socrates? Don't you remember how he sent Xanthippe away on the day on which he was to die, so that his mind should not to be perturbed?"

"Don't talk to me about that either! I refuse to believe that that story of Plato's is anything more than a novel —— "

"Or a *nivola* —— "

"Just as you like."

And brusquely cutting short the delight of conversation, he took his leave.

In the street a beggar approached him and said: "Blessed be the Lord! señorito, alms; I have seven children."

"You ought not to have them," replied Augusto sharply.

"I should like to see what you would do in my place," replied the beggar. "What do you expect us poor people to do if we don't have children — for the rich?"

"You're quite right," replied Augusto. "And for being a philosopher — here, take this!" And he gave him a peseta, which the good man went off at once to spend in the nearest tavern.

XXIII

*P*OOR Augusto was in a state of dismay. It was not merely that he found himself in the position of the ass of Buridanus, attracted equally by Eugenia and by Rosario. The trouble was that the temptation to fall in love with every woman that he saw, instead of growing weaker, was growing stronger. He was beginning to feel that he was fated.

"Go away, Liduvina, go away, for Lord's sake! Go away and leave me by myself! Run along! Out with you!" — once he found himself saying to his servant.

And when she had left he rested his elbows on the table, his head in the palms of his hands, and he said to himself: "This is terrible! Really, this is terrible! It seems that unwittingly I am falling in love — with Liduvina! Poor Domingo! There's no doubt about it. In spite of her fifty years she is still good-looking and round and plump; and when she comes out of the kitchen with her sleeves rolled up and her round arms — come, this is madness! And that double chin and the folds in her neck! Oh! but this is terrible —— "

"Come here, Orfeo," he continued, picking up the dog. "What do you think I ought to do? How am I going to defend myself until I make up my mind and marry? Ah, now I have it! An idea, a brilliant idea, Orfeo! Let us convert this matter of woman, which is now tormenting me, into a subject-matter for study. What do you say to my devoting myself to the psychology of woman? Yes, I will write two monographs — since monographs are very much in style just now. One of them will be entitled, 'Eugenia,' and the other, 'Rosario'; and the sub-title of each will be, 'A study of Woman.' What do you think of my idea, Orfeo?"

He decided, then, to go and consult Antolín S. (i. e., Sánchez) Paparrigópolus who at that time was devoting himself to a study of women, though rather more of women in books than in life.

Antolín S. Paparrigópulos was one of those persons who are known as erudites — a young man destined to bring days of glory to his country by dilucidating the most neglected glories of her past. If the name of Antolín S. Paparrigópulos was not yet heard among those of the ebullient youth who sought to attract the attention of the public by the power of noise, this was because he possessed the truer and deeper quality of power, namely, patience; and because his respect for the public and for himself was such that he was deferring the

hour of his public appearance until, his preparation completed, he felt sure of the ground he was
treading.

So far from seeking a tinsel and ephemeral
reputation, built upon the ignorance of others, by
indulging in this or in that harlequinesque novelty,
he aspired, in all the works of literature that he
was planning, to realize the sum of perfection that
was humanly possible; and above all else to keep
within the boundaries of good sense and of good
taste. Unwilling to strike a false note for the sake
of making himself heard, it was his purpose rather
to reinforce, with a voice carefully trained, the
glorious harmony of a literary tradition genuinely
national and pure-bred.

S. Paparrigópulos was endowed with a clear
intelligence. Above everything else it was clear;
and indeed of a transparency truly marvellous,
undimmed by any species of vagueness or nebu-
losity. He thought always in clear Castilian, free
alike from the influence of horrid northern fogs
and from any taint of the decadence of the Pari-
sian boulevards — in a Castilian perfectly clean and
pure. And therefore, because his thinking was
done with the soul of the race which nourished it,
and from which his own spirit was drawn, his
thought was solid and deep. Hyperborean mists
might be well enough for drinkers of reinforced
beer, but not in this most illustrious Spain of ours,

with her resplendent sky, and her wholesome wine of Valdepeñas, treated with lime! His philosophy was that of the unfortunate Becerro de Bengoa who, after calling Schopenhauer a crazy old bird, made the statement that it would not have occurred to Schopenhauer to say what he did, nor would he have been a pessimist, if he had drunk Valdepeñas instead of beer — and who also said that neurasthenia comes from not minding one's own business and that the cure for it is donkey-feed.

Convinced that in the last analysis the essence of all things is form — a more or less inner form — and that the universe itself is only a kaleidoscope of forms fitted each into the other, and that it is because of their form that the great works preserved through the centuries are still alive, S. Paparrigópolus labored with all the zeal of those marvellous artificers of the Renaissance to perfect the language in which he was to clothe his future works.

He had had the laudable firmness to stand unshaken by any of the currents of neo-romantic sentimentalism. Nor had he yielded to that fashionable but devastating interest in what are called social questions. Convinced that the social question is insoluble down here, that there will always be rich and poor, and that no mitigation of the

situation is to be expected except that furnished
by the charity of the rich and the resignation of
the poor, he held his mind aloof from disputes that
lead to nothing useful and took refuge in the pure
region of immaculate art, beyond the hurly-burly
of the passions, where man finds a sure retreat and
consolation for the disappointments of life. Fur-
thermore, he detested that sterile cosmopolitanism
which merely stupefies the mind with impotent
dreams and enervating Utopias, and he loved and
idolized this Spain of ours, so calumniated by her
children and so little known by them! This Spain
which was to supply him with the original material
for the works upon which his future fame would
rest.

Paparrigópulos had dedicated the mighty en-
ergies of his mind to an investigation of the inner
life of our people in the past, and his work was as
self-denying as it was solid. He aspired to nothing
less than a resuscitation of our past in the eyes of
his compatriots — a resuscitation of the present of
their forbears! And being fully cognizant of the
deceptions suffered by those who have attempted
this by the simple exercise of imagination, he de-
voted himself to research, and to repeated research,
covering the whole field of ancient documents and
memoirs, so that the edifice of his erudite science of
history should rise upon foundations once and for

all immovable. There was no event of the past, however seemingly insignificant, which had not in his eyes an inestimable value.

He knew that one must learn to see the universe in a drop of water; that the paleontologist reconstructs the whole of an animal from a single bone, and the archeologist the whole of an ancient civilization from the handle of a pitcher. Yet he did not forget, on the other hand, that one must not view the stars through a microscope or the infusoria through a telescope — a trick practiced by those humourists who like to see things confused. But although he knew that the handle of a pitcher sufficed to enable an archeological genius to reconstruct a whole world of art buried in the limbo of oblivion, yet since, very modestly, he did not regard himself as a genius, he preferred two pitcher-handles to one — and the more handles the better — and he preferred the whole pitcher to the handle alone.

"Whatever is gained in extension is lost in intensiveness" — this was his motto. Paparrigópulos never forgot that an entire philosophy may be revealed in a most specialized piece of work, and in a monograph upon a topic most constricted. And above everything else he believed in the miracles wrought by the division of labor; and in the enormous progress contributed to science by the self-denying legion of bug-stickers, word-chasers, date-guessers, and drop-computers.

What most appealed to him, and held his attention, were those highly arduous and delicate problems connected with the history of our literature, such as the question of the native land of Prudencio. Of late, however, in consequence, it was whispered, of having been rejected in marriage, he had been devoting himself to a study of Spanish women of past centuries.

It was in works of a character seemingly most insignificant that one could best perceive and admire the acuteness, the good sense, the perspicacity, the marvellous intuition and critical penetration of S. Paparrigópulos. To form a just notion of his qualities it was necessary to see them thus, applied to the concrete, to the living object, and not dissipated in the abstract region of pure theory; one had to catch him in the act. Every one of those dissertations of his was a complete course in inductive logic, a monument of investigation as marvellous as the work of Lionnet on the cress-rocket; and above all a demonstration of what is meant by the austere love of sacred Truth. Ingeniousness he shunned as one shuns the plague; and he believed that only by training ourselves to respect divine Truth in the smallest detail shall we learn to give her due homage in the large.

Among other things he was engaged in the preparation of a popular edition of the apologues of Kalilah and Dimnah, with an introduction treating of the influence of Indian literature upon Spain in the Middle Ages. Would that he had reached the point of publishing it! For undoubtedly it would have resulted in drawing our people away from the taverns and in distracting their attention from pernicious doctrines advocating impossible economic reforms. Of the two great works, however, which Paparrigópulos was planning, the first was a history of obscure Spanish writers; of those, in other words, who are either not mentioned at all in current histories of literature or receive only a passing mention, owing to the assumed unimportance of their works. In this work he aimed to remedy the injustice of the times, an injustice which he not only deplored, but also feared. The second work treated of those authors whose writings have been lost, leaving us with only a record of their names or at most of the titles of their works. But he was also about to undertake a history of that third class of authors who, having thought of writing, had never reached the point of doing so.

For the better success of his undertakings, Paparrigópulos, after once being sufficiently nourished upon the substantial meat of our national literature, had taken a bath in foreign literatures. And since he found this a rather painful task —

for he was slow in learning foreign tongues, and
the study of them demanded time needed for
higher pursuits — he resorted to a notable expe-
dient which he had learned from a distinguished
master. He read the principal works of criticism
and literary history published in foreign countries
— whenever they could be found in French trans-
lation — and having gathered the average opinion
of the most reputable critics regarding this author
or that, he spent a few moments turning the pages
of the author's works; thereby satisfying his conscience and at the same time putting himself in a
position to make over the opinions of others with
no prejudice to his own scrupulous integrity as a
critic.

It will be seen, then, that S. Paparrigópulos
was not one of those vagrant and erratic young
spirits who, with no fixed aim, saunter idly through
the domains of thought and fancy, striking here
and there a fugitive spark. No! His tendencies were
rigorously and solidly pedestrian: he was one of
those who are going somewhere. If there should
seem to be nothing outstanding in the field of his
accomplishments, this would be due to the fact
that the whole field formed a summit, after the
fashion of a plateau; thus presenting a faithful
image of our vast sunburnt Castilian plains, wav-
ing with golden nourishing wheat.

Oh, that Providence would send us many more

Antolín Sánchez Paparrigópuloses! With their aid
we should make ourselves masters of our fund of
tradition and thus gather from it a richer harvest.
When Paparrigópulos aspired (and he is still aspir-
ing, since he is still living and still engaged in the
preparation of his works) — when Paparrigópulos
aspired to penetrate the soil with his critical
ploughshare, though only a centimetre deeper than
the ploughmen who had preceded him in the field,
it was with the idea that, thanks to the juices derived from deeper sources of moisture, the wheat
would grow more luxuriantly, the spikes would be
more heavily grained, the flour richer in quality,
and we Spaniards should then feed upon a spiritual
bread both better and cheaper.

It has just been said that Paparrigópulos is
still engaged in the task of preparing his works for
the light of publication. Such indeed is the fact.
And though he had then published nothing, and
has published nothing yet, it happened that
through friends whom they had in common, Augusto had heard of the studies of women to which
Paparrigópulos was devoting himself.

There are not wanting other erudites who,
with the generosity characteristic of their kind,
having caught sight of Paparrigópulos, and being
envious from the start of the fame that they see
awaiting him, are attempting to belittle him. One
of them says of Paparrigópulos that, like the fox,

he brushes out his tracks with his tail and exe-
cutes so many twists and turns in various directions
that he throws the hunters off the track, and no
one knows where he expected to capture the hen;
and that if he has any one fault it is that of leaving
the scaffold standing after the tower has been completed, so as to prevent us either from admiring
the structure or from seeing what it is. Another
speaks of him disdainfully as a mere commentator
— as if commentary were not a supreme form of
art! Still another accuses him, now of merely trans-
lating, or again of merely adapting ideas taken
from foreign literature — forgetting that when
Paparrigópulos reclothes these ideas in a Castilian
so clear, so limpid, and so pure-bred as his own, he
makes the ideas themselves Castilian, and properly
his own ideas, in just the fashion that Padre Isla
made his own the *Gil Blas* of Le Sage. Another
chaffs him by saying that his principal resource is
his deep faith in the ignorance of the public — he
who judges him thus forgetting all the while that
faith moves mountains. But the supreme injustice
to be charged against these and other begrudging
opinions of people whom Paparrigópulos has never
harmed in the least, the most notorious injustice
— this will be easily clear to those who remember
that Paparrigópulos has thus far laid nothing before the public, and therefore that those who are
now howling and biting at his heels are talking

from mere hearsay and only for the pleasure of saying something.

In a word, it is not possible to write of this distinguished erudite with other than a feeling of serene satisfaction. And surely there is nothing about him to justify a characterization in the least "nivolistic."

And so this was the man — I mean that this was the erudite — of whom Augusto was thinking, having heard that he was devoting himself to studies of women — to studies of women in books, let us remember, where they can be studied with the least danger to the student, and of women of past centuries, who, on the other hand, are least exposed to danger from the student himself.

This Antolín, then, a solitary erudite who studied women in books because he was too timid to resort to them in life, and because he wished to get his revenge for this timidity — he it was to whom Augusto hastened in search of advice.

Hardly had he explained his errand when the erudite interrupted him:

"Alas, my poor Señor Pérez, how I pity you! You wish to study women? A most difficult task, I can assure you —— "

"But you are studying them yourself —— "

"Yes, one must make the sacrifice. And as for me, the function of research, of silent, patient, and inconspicuous research, is the one reason for being

in my life. But then you know that I am only a
day-labourer, a very humble labourer, in the field
of thought; one of those who gather and arrange
the materials for those who will later know how to
make use of them. All human work is collective:
nothing that is not collective is ever solid or dur-
able —— "

"But what of the works of the great men of
genius — *The Divine Comedy*, the *Æneid*, a
tragedy of Shakespeare, a painting of Velaz-
quez? —— "

"All of it is collective, and much more collective than anyone suspects. *The Divine Comedy*, for
example, had the foundation laid for it in a whole
series of —— "

"Yes, I know all about that."

"And in regard to Velasquez — by the way,
are you acquainted with Justi's book about him?"

In the eyes of Antolín the principal importance, almost the only importance indeed, of the
great masterworks of human genius lay in having
called forth a commentary or a work of criticism.
The great artists, poets, painters, musicians, his-
torians, philosophers, were born for the purpose of
having an erudite write their biography or a critic
write a commentary on their works. Take any passage you please from the works of a great writer, it
acquires significance only when it is quoted by an
erudite who cites the passage, with the edition and

the page upon which it appears. All of that talk
about the solidarity of collective effort was the expression, really, of envy and impotence. Paparrigópulos belonged in the same class with those com-
mentators on Homer who, if Homer himself should
appear again in the flesh and enter their offices singing his *Iliad,* would shoot him out again forthwith,
because he disturbed them in the task of searching
through the dead texts of his poems for words oc-
curring only once.

"But tell me, then, what is your view of the
psychology of women?"

"A question of that sort, so vague, so general,
so abstract, is wholly lacking in precise meaning for
a modest investigator like me, friend Pérez — for
a man who is neither a genius nor desires to be
one —— "

"Nor desires to be one?"

"No, I have no desire to be one. It is a poor
part to play. And so for me this question of yours
is lacking in precise meaning. To answer your question it would be necessary to —— "

"Yes, I see, to do as was done by a colleague of
yours who wrote a book on the psychology of the
Spanish people. Living among Spaniards and being, it seems, a Spaniard himself, all that he could
think of was to say that this man says this and the
other man says that, and to construct a bibliography —— "

"Ah, a bibliography! Yes, now I see —— "

"No, friend Paparrigópulos, never mind about that. Please tell me as concretely as you know how what your opinion is concerning the psychology of women."

"We should have to begin by basing our inquiry upon a preliminary question, namely, whether woman has a soul."

"Come!"

"Ah, but there is no use of dismissing the question in that fashion — so summarily —— "

"Can he himself have a soul?" thought Augusto; and then he said:

"Very well, then. But now, speaking only of what takes the place of soul in women — what do you think of that?"

"Will you promise me, friend Pérez, to keep the secret of what I am going to tell you? However, no! There's no danger; you are not an erudite."

"What do you imply by that?"

"I mean that you are not one of those who are ready to rob a man of anything they have just heard him say and then give it out as their own —— "

"But do you mean that this kind of thing —— ?"

"Alas! friend Pérez, the erudite is by nature a pickpocket. And it is I who tell you so, I who am one of them. We erudites spend our time in stealing from one another the little discoveries that we make and in guarding ourselves against those who would get ahead of us."

"One can easily understand that. The proprietor of a warehouse watches over his goods more zealously than the proprietor of a mill. It's the water in the well that has to be saved, not the water of the flood."

"Perhaps so. Well, then, if you who are not an erudite will promise to keep my secret until I reveal it myself, I will tell you that in an obscure and nearly unknown Dutch writer of the seventeenth century I have found a most interesting theory concerning the soul of woman —— "

"Let's hear it."

"Says this writer — and he says it in Latin — that while every man has a soul of his own, all the women taken together have but one and the same soul, something like the active understanding of Averroes, which is shared by them all. And he adds that the differences observed in the manner of feeling, thinking, and willing among women are due, not to the soul, but to bodily differences — which may be attributed to race, climate, nourishment and the like — all of which explains why these differences are so trifling and insignificant. Women, this writer says, are much more alike than men are;

and this is because they are all together only one
and the same woman —— "

"Now I have it, friend Paparrigópulos! This
explains why, as soon as I fell in love with one
woman, I at once felt myself in love with all the
rest."

"That's perfectly clear! And then this most
interesting and nearly unknown gynecologist goes
on to say that women have much more individual-
ity than men, but much less personality. Any
woman feels that she is more exclusively herself,
more of an individual, than any man does; but she
feels herself poorer in content."

"Yes, yes, I think I make out what he means."

"And therefore, friend Pérez, it makes no difference whether you study one woman or several.
The point is to go deeply into the study of the
woman that you select."

"But would it not be better to select two or
more, so as to make it a comparative study? For
you know that comparative studies are very much
the thing just now —— "

"Very true. Science is indeed a method of
comparison. But in the study of women comparison is unnecessary. He who knows one of them, and
knows her well, knows them all; he knows Woman.
Moreover, you know that whatever is gained in
extension is lost in intensiveness."

"Of course. And I wish to devote myself to the intensive cultivation of women, and not to the extensive. But to at least two, I should say — at least two —— "

"No, not to two! On no account! If you cannot be content to study one — which seems to me to be the better plan, and certainly enough of a task — then you must study at least three. Duality is inconclusive."

"Duality inconclusive? How is that?"

"It's very simple. Two lines cannot enclose an area of space. The simplest polygon is a triangle. And so, at least three."

"But the triangle is without volume. The simplest polyhedron is a tetrahedron; and that means at least four."

"But not two! Never! If more than one, then at least three. But I advise you to go deeply into the study of one."

"That is my intention."

XXIV

On the way home from the inter-
view with Paparrigópulos Augusto said to himself: "It seems, then, that I shall have to drop one
of the two or look for a third. However, for the
purposes of my psychological study Liduvina can
very well serve as the third term — of course as
a purely theoretical third term, merely for the sake
of comparison. And so I have three: Eugenia, who
appeals to my imagination, that is, to my head;
Rosario, who appeals to my heart; and Liduvina,
my cook, who appeals to my stomach. And head,
heart, and stomach — these are the three faculties
of the soul which other persons call intelligence,
feeling, and will. We think with the head, feel with
the heart, and desire with the stomach. So far it's
all beautifully clear! And now ——

"And now —— " he continued. "Ah, a brilliant, a dazzling idea! I am going to pretend that I
wish to renew the affair with Eugenia and then
court her again, to see if she will accept me as her
fiancé and future husband. Only to test her, of
course — just by way of experiment. For I am certain that she will reject me. Think of her doing
anything else! She is compelled to reject me. After

all that has happened, after what she said to me at our last meeting, it is not possible for her to accept me now. She's a woman of her word, I am certain. But — is it a fact that women have a word? Is it true that Woman — Woman with a capital W, the one Woman, shared by millions of feminine bodies more or less beautiful — and rather more than less — is it true that Woman is obliged to keep her word? This business of keeping one's word, isn't it perhaps distinctly masculine? But no, no! Eugenia can't accept me because she doesn't love me. She doesn't love me, and besides she has now accepted my gift. And if she has accepted the gift and is enjoying the benefit of it, what is she going to love me for?

"But," it occurred to him presently, "suppose that she does go back on what she has said and says 'Yes' and accepts me as her fiancé and future husband? For it is well to face all the possibilities. What if she accepts me, I say? If she does, I'm in a deuce of a mess. To think of her catching me with my own hook! That would certainly be a case of hooking the angler! But no! no! it can't possibly be! Yet suppose it were! Ah! Then the only thing to do is to be resigned. One must know how to be resigned to good fortune. Yet it may be that to know how to be resigned to happiness is just the hardest thing of all to learn. Doesn't Pindar tell us that all of the misfortunes of Tantalus arose from his not being able to digest his happiness? Yes, one must digest one's happiness! And if Eugenia says 'Yes' and accepts me, then — then hurrah for psychology! Psychology has won! But no, no, no! She won't accept me, she simply can't. She will reject me if only to have her own way. You can't put anything over on a woman like Eugenia. When Woman faces Man with the idea of showing him which of them has the greater constancy and tenacity of purpose, she is capable of anything. No, she won't accept me!"

"Rosario is waiting for you."

With these simple words, pregnant with possibilities of emotion, Liduvina interrupted the current of her master's reflections.

"Tell me, Liduvina, do you believe that women stand by what they have once said? Do you women know how to keep your word?"

"It all depends."

"Yes, that's the everlasting refrain of your husband. But give me a straight answer — not the kind that women usually give. For you women very seldom reply to the question that one asks you, but always to the question that you thought one was going to ask."

"And what was it that you wanted to ask me?"

"This. When you women have given your word do you stand by it?"

"It depends on the word."

"What do you mean by that?"

"Why, it's simple enough. Some words are given to be kept and others not to be kept. And nobody is deceived, because it's all understood."

"Very well, that's enough! Now tell Rosario to come in."

"Tell me, Rosario, what do you think, ought a woman to stand by the word that she has given or not?"

"I don't remember having given you my word about anything —— "

"That isn't the question. The question is whether a woman ought or ought not to keep the word she has given —— "

"Oh, I see. You are thinking about the other woman — about that woman —— "

"Never mind what I am thinking about. Tell me what you think."

"But I don't understand such things very well —— "

"That makes no difference."

"Well, seeing that I have to give you an answer, I think it is better not to give your word about anything."

"But what if you have already given your word?"

"Shouldn't have done it."

"It's plain to be seen," said Augusto to himself, "that this child can't be budged. But now that she is here, I'll bring psychology into play and carry out an experiment."

"Come on over, sit down here!" — and he offered his knee.

The girl obeyed him calmly, without the slightest change of countenance, as if it were something foreseen and agreed upon. Augusto, on the contrary, became confused and knew not where to begin his psychological investigation. And since he knew nothing to say, well — he acted. He pressed Rosario to his heaving breast and covered her face with kisses, saying to himself meanwhile: "It seems that I am about to lose the composure which is necessary for psychological experiment." Suddenly he checked himself, seemed to grow calmer, relaxed his hold upon Rosario, and said to her abruptly:

"But don't you know that I love another woman?"

Rosario was silent. She looked him steadily in the face and shrugged her shoulders.

"But don't you know it?" he repeated.

"What difference does that make to me now ——"

"Why doesn't it make a difference?"

"Now? Not now. Just now it seems to me that you love me."

"And it seems so to me too, but —— "

And then something extraordinary took place, something that Augusto had neither foreseen nor provided for in his program for the psychological investigation of Woman. Without warning Rosario clasped her arms around his neck and began to kiss him. The poor man had barely time for the thought, "It is I who am being experimented upon now; this maiden is carrying out studies in masculine psychology." Hardly knowing what he was doing, he was surprised to find his trembling hand caressing the calf of her leg.

Suddenly Augusto rose, lifted Rosario up bodily and laid her on the sofa. She allowed him to do it, with her face aflame. And he, grasping her arms with his hands and holding her down, looked fixedly into her eyes.

"Don't close them, Rosario, don't close them! For heaven's sake, open them! That's the way, that's the way; a little more, a little more! Let me see myself in them, so tiny, so tiny —— "

When he looked in those eyes, as in a living mirror, he felt that his excitement was beginning to subside.

"Let me see myself in them — they're like a mirror. I seem so tiny. Only thus shall I come to know myself — seeing myself in the eyes of a woman —— "

The mirror was looking at him strangely. Rosario was thinking: "This man seems different from the others; he must be mad."

Suddenly he drew away from her, looked at himself, and then felt himself, exclaiming at last:

"Forgive me, Rosario, forgive me."

"Forgive you? For what?"

The tone of poor Rosario's voice was more expressive of fear than of anything else. She felt a desire to escape. For she said to herself, "When a person begins to talk and act as strangely as this, you don't know where he is going to stop. This man might easily kill me in an attack of frenzy." And the tears gushed to her eyes.

"Do you see?" said Augusto. "Do you see? Yes, forgive me, Rosario, forgive me. I didn't know what I was doing."

She thought: "What he doesn't know is — what he didn't do."

"And now go! Be off!"

"Are you driving me away?"

"No, I am defending myself. No, I am not driving you away! God forbid! If you wish I will go away myself and you can stay here, so that you can see that I am not driving you away."

"There's clearly something wrong with him," she thought; and she pitied him.

"Be off! Go! And you won't forget me, will you?" He put his hand to her chin and stroked it. "Don't forget me; don't forget poor Augusto."

He embraced her and gave her a long and lasting kiss on the lips. As the girl went out she gave him a look full of dark, mysterious fear. When she had gone Augusto thought to himself: "She despises me. There's no doubt that she despises me. I was ridiculous, utterly, utterly ridiculous. But after all what does she know about things of this kind, poor child? What does she know about psychology?"

Had poor Augusto been able to read the mind of Rosario at that moment he would have despaired the more. For the innocent maiden was thinking to herself: "It'll be a cold day when I come here to go through this kind of thing again for the benefit of that other woman —— "

Augusto felt his excitement returning. It was beginning to dawn upon him that time once past never returns to offer for a second time the opportunities rejected. He was seized with rage against himself. Hardly knowing what he was doing — just to fill the time in some fashion — he called Liduvina. But when he saw her before him, plump and serene, and smiling mischievously, he was possessed by such an extraordinary feeling that, saying to her, "Be off! Be off! Be off!" he rushed out into the street. For a moment he feared that he would lose control of himself and attack Liduvina.

Once in the street he calmed down. The crowd

is like a grove of trees: it puts each of us back in his place and straightens him out again.

"Can I be right in my head?" Augusto was thinking. "May it not be true that, while I think I am walking properly along the street, like any normal person — and, by the way, what is a normal person? — I am really indulging in pantomimic gesticulations and contortions? And may it not be that these people who seem to be passing without looking at me, or to be looking at me with indifference, really have, all of them, their eyes fixed upon me, either laughing at me or pitying me? But why should I have this idea? Isn't that madness too? Can I really be mad? But supposing that I am, in the last analysis what of it? A man with a heart, a man sensitive and kind, if he doesn't go mad it is because he is utterly stupid. He who is not mad is either a fool or a rogue. Which doesn't mean, of course, that fools and rogues are not crazy too.

"What I did to Rosario — " he continued thinking, "that was ridiculous, absolutely ridiculous! What must she have thought of me? But what difference does it make what a girl of that kind thinks of me? —— Poor child! But — how innocently she let me do it! She is a physiological being, purely and perfectly physiological, devoid of any psychology whatever. There's no use, then, of trying to make her the frog or guinea-pig of psychological experiments. She's good at most for

physiological experiments —— But psychology —
feminine psychology, at any rate — is it really anything more than physiology, or possibly physiological psychology? Has woman a soul? The
difficulty about my engaging in psycho-physical
experiments is that I have no experience in laboratory technique. I never took a single laboratory
course — and besides I have no apparatus. And
psycho-physiology requires apparatus. Can I, then,
be really mad?"

Having relieved his mind by these meditations,
along the street, in the midst of a busy multitude
indifferent to his troubles, he felt himself growing
calmer and returned home.

XXV

A U G U S T O paid a visit to Victor. He wanted to hug his belated son, to refresh his spirit in the contemplation of the happiness newly arrived in that home, and incidentally to consult Victor about the state of his own mind. When he found him alone he said:

"What about that novel — what was it? — ah, yes, that *nivola* that you were writing? I suppose that, now that the boy has arrived, you have given it up."

"Then you suppose wrong. Just for that reason, because I am now a father, I have taken it up again. I find in it an outlet for the happiness that is filling me."

"Would you like to read me some of it?"

Victor brought out the manuscript and began to read to his friend passages here and there.

"But, man, it seems to me that this makes you out a different sort of person!" exclaimed Augusto.

"How?"

"Why, there are things here that border on the obscene, and at times they cross the border —— "

"Obscene? Not for a moment. You will find some things here that are rather raw, but nothing obscene. Now and then a nude, but never anyone disrobed. What you see here is realism —— "

"Realism, yes; and on top of that —— "

"Cynicism. Isn't that it?"

"Yes, cynicism."

"But cynicism is not the same thing as obscenity. These crudities of mine are only a method of rousing the imagination in such a way as to lead it to a more discerning examination of the realities of things. They are — pedagogical crudities. That's the word — pedagogical!"

"And somewhat grotesque —— "

"Quite true. I don't deny it. I delight in buffooneries."

"Of the kind that are always at bottom rather dismal."

"That is just why I enjoy them. It is only the lugubrious jokes that please me, and the funereal jests. Laughter for the sake of laughter shocks me and almost terrifies me. Laughter is properly only a preparation for tragedy."

"Well, these crude buffooneries of yours seem detestable to me and leave me with a very unpleasant feeling."

"That is because you are a solitary person, Augusto — you understand me, solitary and celibate. And I write these things to serve as a cure ——

No, I have no purpose at all in writing them, but only because I find diversion in the writing of them. And if those who read them find them diverting that is all that I ask for. But if at the same time I succeed by their means in starting on the road to recovery some poor solitary fellow like you, suffering from a double solitude —— "

"Double solitude?"

"Yes, solitude of body and solitude of soul."

"Apropos, Victor —— "

"Yes, I know what you are going to tell me. You have come to consult me about your state of mind, which has been for some time past alarming, truly alarming. Isn't that true?"

"Yes, it is."

"I guessed so. Well, then, Augusto, marry; and marry as soon as possible."

"Which one?"

"Ah! And so there is more than one?"

"How have you managed to guess that too?"

"Very simply. If you had asked only, 'Whom?' I should not have thought there was more than one, assuming that there was even one. But when you ask, 'Which one?' it is clear that you mean, which one of the two, three, ten, or n."

"True."

"Marry, then; marry! Marry any of the n women with whom you are in love. Marry the one that comes handiest. And don't think too much about it. You see, I married without thinking about it; we were forced to marry."

"But I have just begun to devote myself to an experimental investigation of feminine psychology."

"The one really experimental investigation of Woman is matrimony. A man who is not married will never be able to experiment psychologically upon the soul of Woman. The one laboratory of feminine psychology — or, I should say, of gynecopsychology — is matrimony."

"Yes, but there's no backing out of matrimony."

"There's no backing out of any process of experimentation that is real. A man who decides that he wishes to enter a field of experiment and yet leave open a way of retreat, not burning his boats behind him, will never get any sure knowledge. Never trust yourself to a surgeon who has not amputated a limb of his own; never turn yourself over to an alienist who is not himself mad. Marry, then, if you wish to learn some psychology."

"Which means that bachelors —— "

"What bachelors know is not psychology. It is nothing more than metaphysics — that is to say, something beyond physics, or beyond nature."

"And where's that?"

"Just where you are now."

"Do you mean to say that I am in the region

of metaphysics? My dear Victor, I am not beyond
the natural, but still on this side of it. I have not
yet reached the natural."

"It's the same thing."

"How the same thing?"

"Yes, this side of the natural is the same as
beyond the natural, just as beyond space is the
same as this side of space. Do you see this line?" —
and he drew a line on a piece of paper. "Extend it
to infinity in both directions and the ends will
meet. They will join one another in infinity, where
all things meet and all things are united. Every
straight line is a curve, with an infinite periphery
and an infinite radius, which is closed at infinity.
And therefore this side of the natural is the same
as the other side of the natural. Isn't that clear?"

"No, it is most obscure, very obscure indeed."

"Well, because it is so obscure, then marry!"

"Yes, but — I am assailed by so many doubts."

"All the better, little Hamlet, all the better!
You doubt? Then you think? Then you are."

"Yes, doubting is thinking."

"And thinking is doubting, and nothing but
doubting. One believes, one knows, one imagines,
all without doubting. Neither belief, nor knowledge, nor imagination presupposes doubt. They are
even destroyed by doubt. But one never thinks
without doubting. And it is doubt that converts
belief and knowledge, both of which are static, in-

ert, dead, into thought, which is dynamic, moving, alive."

"Imagination too?"

"Well, there's room for doubt there. I am usually in doubt about what I am going to have the characters of my *nivola* say and do. And even after I have had them say or do something, I doubt whether it was well done, whether it was what suits them. But — I let it stand! Yes, yes, in imagination there's room for doubt, for imagination is thought."

While Augusto and Victor were carrying on this "nivolistic" conversation, I, the author of this nivola *which you, my dear reader, are holding in your hand and reading — I was smiling enigmatically at the sight of my "nivolistic" characters advocating my case and justifying my methods of procedure. And I said to myself, "Think how far these poor fellows are from suspecting that they are only trying to justify what I am doing with them! In the same fashion, whenever a man is seeking for reasons wherewith to justify himself, he is, strictly speaking, only seeking to justify God. And I am the God of these two poor 'nivolistic' devils."*

XXVI

A U G U S T O directed his steps to the home of Eugenia, prepared for the last of his series of psychological experiments, which was to be definitive; fearing all the while, however, that she might repulse him. He met her on the steps. She was coming down on her way out as he ascended on his way in.

"You here, Don Augusto?"

"Yes, it is I. But since you are obliged to go out I will let it go until another day. I will come again."

"No, don't go. My uncle is at home."

"But it is not your uncle that I wanted to see, Eugenia, but you. Let's leave it for another day."

"No, no, let's go up again. Strike the iron while it is hot."

"But if your uncle is at home —— "

"Bah! He's an anarchist. We won't call him."

And she compelled Augusto to mount the stairs with her. The poor man who had set out with all the airs of an experimenter now began to feel that in this experiment he was playing the part of the frog.

When they were alone in the drawing-room

Eugenia said to him — she was still dressed for the street and had not removed her hat — "Very well. Let's hear what it is that you had to say to me."

"Why — why — " stammered poor Augusto, "why — why —— "

"Yes, but why what?"

"Eugenia, I can't get any rest. I have turned over and over in my mind, a thousand times, what we said the last time we spoke to each other, and after doing my best, I can't become resigned. No, I cannot resign myself, I simply can't!"

"And what is it to which you can't resign yourself?"

"Why, to this, Eugenia, to this!"

"And what do you mean by 'this'?"

"Why, to this — to our being nothing more than friends —— "

"Nothing more than friends! Does that seem to you a small matter, Señor Don Augusto? Or is it that you wish us to be something less than friends?"

"No, Eugenia, no; nothing of that kind."

"What is it, then?"

"Heavens, don't make me suffer —— "

"It is you who are making yourself suffer."

"I can't resign myself. I simply can't."

"But what is it that you want?"

"I want — I want us to be man and wife!"

"Let us have done with that!"

"To have done with it we must first begin."

"But what of the promise you made me?"

"I didn't know what I was saying —— "

"And what of that girl, Rosario?"

"O Lord, Eugenia, don't remind me of that! Stop thinking about Rosario!"

Eugenia rose, took off her hat and laid it upon a small table. She returned to her seat and then, speaking slowly and solemnly, said:

"Very well, then, Augusto. Now that you, who are after all a man, think that you are no longer obliged to keep your word, I, who am only a woman, am not bound to keep mine either. Besides, I want to free you from Rosario and from the other Rosarios or Petras who are likely to entangle you. That which gratitude for your gift could not do, or bitterness for what happened to me in connection with Mauricio — you can see whether I am not frank with you — has been brought about by pity. Yes, Augusto, it pains me to think of you, it pains me deeply!" — and as she said this she gave him two light pats on the knee with her right hand.

"Eugenia!" and he held out his arms to embrace her.

"Ah? Be careful! Careful!" she cried, moving away out of his reach.

"But the other time — the last time —— "

"Yes, but then it was different!"

"I am playing the part of the frog," thought the experimental psychologist.

"Yes," Eugenia continued, "to a friend who is nothing more than a friend one may permit certain small liberties which one ought not to grant to a — well, to a fiancé!"

"But I don't see why —— "

"After we are married, Augusto, I will explain it to you. But now you are going to behave, aren't you?"

"The thing is settled," thought Augusto, who now felt perfectly and completely the frog.

"And now," said Eugenia, rising as she spoke, "I'm going to call my uncle."

"What for?"

"Why, to tell him about it."

"Yes, of course!" cried Augusto utterly dismayed.

Don Fermín appeared in a moment.

"I have something to say to you, Uncle," said Eugenia. "Here is Don Augusto Pérez who has come to ask for my hand. And I have granted it to him."

"Splendid! Splendid!" cried Don Fermín. "Wonderful! Come here, daughter, come here and let me embrace you. Wonderful!"

"Does it seem to you so wonderful, Uncle, that we are going to be married?"

"No, not just that. What I admire — what I

wonder at, what overcomes me — is the way you have managed this business, the two of you alone, without any go-between. Hurrah for anarchy! It's a pity, a great pity, that you can't carry out your plan without resorting to authority — but of course you will disregard authority in the inner tribunal of your consciousness. It's a matter of form, is it not? Simply a matter of form. For I know that you already consider yourselves to be man and wife. And in any case, on my own authority I, in the name of the anarchical God, hereby join you in wedlock. And that is all that is necessary. Wonderful! Wonderful! Don Augusto, henceforth this house is yours."

"Henceforth?"

"I beg your pardon. Yes, to be sure, it was always yours. My house — mine? Well, this house that I live in was always yours; it belonged always to all my brothers. But henceforth — well, you understand me."

"Yes, Uncle, he understands you."

At that moment there was a knock at the door, and Eugenia cried, "My aunt!" As she entered the room and grasped the situation, she exclaimed, "Ah, I see. And so it is all settled, is it? I knew that it was."

Augusto kept thinking: "Frog! Frog! Absolutely the frog! Among them all, they have hooked me nicely."

"Of course you will stay and dine with us today, to celebrate the occasion," said Doña Ermelinda.

"What else can I do?" broke from the lips of the poor frog.

XXVII

T H E N began a new life for Augusto. He spent nearly the whole day at his fiancée's home, studying now, not psychology, but æsthetics.

And Rosario? Rosario did not come to his house again. The next time it was some other woman that brought his clothes home. Nor did he venture to ask why Rosario had stopped coming. He could easily guess — why should he ask? As for her contempt, for clearly it was contempt, he understood that well enough; but so far from wounding him, it almost pleased him. Let it stand! He would be well repaid for that by having Eugenia. Eugenia, to be sure, had not departed from the rule of, "Ah! Be careful! Hands off!" But she had other attractions.

Eugenia restricted him to an allowance of seeing her, and only of seeing her, thus kindling his passion all the more. Once he said to her:

"I have a great desire to write a few verses to your eyes."

And she replied: "Write them if you like."

"But," he added, "you ought to be playing the piano. Hearing you on your chosen instrument would give me the proper inspiration."

"But you know, Augusto, that since I have stopped giving music lessons, thanks to your generosity, I have never touched the piano again. And I hate it. It had been such a burden to me!"

"Never mind, play it, Eugenia. Play it to help me write my verses."

"Very well, but only this once."

Eugenia seated herself at the piano, and while she was playing Augusto wrote the following:

My soul wandered far from my body
Lost in the mists of the spirit,
Lost yonder among notes of the music
Sung, as they say, by the spheres;
And alone my body lay soulless
And sadly roamed in the world.
Born to labour through life together
They lived not; for he was matter,
Thus alone, and she no more than spirit,
Sweet Eugenia, seeking completeness.
But thine eyes gushed forth like springs
Of living light on my path,
And they captured my soul and brought her
From vague heaven to doubtful earth;
To my body they joined her, and since then,
Since then only, Eugenia, I've lived.
Thine eyes are like fiery nails
Which hold fast my body and soul,
Cause my blood to dream hotly within me,
And convert my ideas into flesh.

If this light of my life were extinguished,
Spirit and matter unyoked,
I were lost in the mists of heaven,
And the hungry night of the deep.

"How do they strike you," asked Augusto
when she had finished reading them.

"Like my piano. Little or no music in them.
And this thing of 'as they say' —— "

"Yes, that's to give a touch of familiarity."

"And that 'Sweet Eugenia'! — that seems to
me rubbish."

"What! Do you mean that you are rubbish?"

"Yes, in these verses! But the whole thing
seems to me very — very —— "

"I know what you mean — 'nivolesque.' "

"What's that?"

"Oh, nothing. Only a little gag that Victor
and I have between us."

"Well, look here, Augusto! After we are married I don't want any gags in my house. Do you
understand that? Neither gags nor dogs. And
therefore you had better be thinking about what
you are going to do with Orfeo —— "

"But Eugenia! Goodness! You know how I
found him, the poor little beggar! And besides, you
know that he's my confidant — why, it is he to
whom I address all my monologues!"

"There are not going to be any monologues in

my house after we are married. The dog is too
much!"

"Heavens, Eugenia! At any rate until we have
a child —— "

"If we have any —— "

"If we have any, of course! But if not, why
not the dog? Why not the dog — of whom it has
been so justly said that he would be man's greatest
friend if he had money —— ?"

"No, if he had money he wouldn't be man's
friend, I am certain of that. He's man's friend because he hasn't money."

On another occasion Eugenia said to Augusto:

"Augusto, there's something important, something very important, that I must speak to you
about, and I ask you to forgive me in advance if
what I am going to say to you —— "

"My Lord, Eugenia, speak!"

"You remember my former fiancé —— "

"Yes, Mauricio."

"But you don't know why I had to get rid of
the shameless creature —— "

"I don't want to know."

"That is splendid of you. Well, I had to dismiss
the impudent loafer, but —— "

"What! Is he still pursuing you?"

"Still!"

"Ah, how I should like to get hold of him!"

"No, no, it's nothing of that kind. He is pursuing me, but not with the intention you suspect, but with other intentions."

"What intentions? Tell me quickly."

"Don't be alarmed, Augusto; there's no cause for alarm. Poor Mauricio doesn't bite, he only barks."

"Oh, then you had better follow the advice given in the Arabic saying: 'If you stop for every dog that runs out and barks at you on the road you will never get to the end of it.' There's no use of throwing stones at him. Don't pay any attention to him."

"I think there's a better way than that."

"What is it?"

"To provide ourselves with pieces of bread and carry them in our pockets and then throw them out as we go along to the dogs that run out and bark at us; for they are barking only because they are hungry."

"What do you mean?"

"I mean this. Mauricio is not asking for anything now except to have me find him a position of some sort, or some way of making his living; and then he will leave me in peace. And if I don't —— "

"Well?"

"He threatens to keep after me and compromise me —— "

"The shameless scoundrel!"

"Don't get excited. I think it is better to get him out of the way by finding him a position that will support him and take him as far away from us as possible. Besides, I feel some pity for the poor fellow. After all, he is what he is, and ——— "

"Perhaps you are right, Eugenia. And I say, I think I can manage it all. I'll see a friend of mine tomorrow, and I think we shall find a job for him."

As it happened, he was able to find the job and to arrange that Mauricio should be sent far enough away.

XXVIII

O N E morning Liduvina announced to Augusto that a young man was waiting to see him. Augusto made a wry face when he learned that it was Mauricio. His first impulse was to send him away without seeing him, but a certain attraction drew him to the man who had once been Eugenia's lover; whom she had loved, and perhaps in some fashion still loved; the man who very likely had enjoyed a more intimate acquaintance with the woman who was now to be his wife, and knew more of her, than he himself; the man who —— There was a bond between them.

"I have come, señor," Mauricio opened the conversation in a tone of deep respect, "to thank you for the distinguished favour which, thanks to the good offices of Eugenia, you have seen fit to grant me —— "

"It is not necessary to thank me, my dear sir; but I hope that in the future you will leave the woman who is to be my wife in peace."

"But surely I have not molested her in the least!"

"I know what I am talking about."

"Since she dismissed me — and she did well to dismiss me, for I am not the man who is suitable for her — I have sought only, as best I could, to console myself for my misfortune and to respect her decision. And if she has told you anything to the contrary —— "

"I must beg you not to refer again to the woman who is to be my wife. And above all I must beg you not even to insinuate that she has departed from the truth in the slightest detail. Console yourself as best you can and leave us in peace."

"I will do so. And again I thank both of you for the favour you have done in getting me this employment. I am going off to take the position and I shall console myself as best I can. To be sure, I am thinking of taking a little girl along with me —— "

"But what business is that of mine, sir?"

"Why, I have an idea that you must know her —— "

"What! What do you mean? Are you trying to be facetious?"

"No, no. She is a girl named Rosario. She is employed in a laundry, and I think she used to bring home your washing —— "

Augusto turned pale. "Can it be that the fellow knows all about it?" he asked himself. This disturbed him even more than the suspicion of a few moments before, that this man knew Eugenia more

intimately than he. But he recovered himself
quickly and exclaimed:

"What brings you with this story to me?"

"It seems to me" — Mauricio went on as if
he had heard nothing — "that we who are despised
and rejected should be left the privilege of consoling one another."

"But what do you mean, man? Say what you
mean." For a second Augusto considered whether
— here upon the scene of his last adventure with
Rosario — he should not strangle the fellow.

"Don't get so excited, Don Augusto; don't get
so excited! I mean only what I have said. She —
she whom you wish me not to mention, she despised me and rejected me, and then I met this
poor child, who had been despised by someone else,
and ——— "

Augusto could no longer contain himself.
Turning first pale and then fiery red, he rose,
grasped Mauricio by his two arms, lifted him into
the air and flung him upon the sofa — all without
knowing what he was doing — as if he were prepared to strangle him. Thereupon Mauricio, having
landed upon the sofa, said with the utmost calmness:

"Look at yourself in my eyes now, Don Augusto, and you will see how tiny you look ——— "

Poor Augusto felt himself dissolving away. At
any rate, all the strength melted out of his arms

and the room turned into a mist before his eyes. "Can I be dreaming this?" he thought. And then he discovered that Mauricio, standing on his feet before him, was looking at him and smiling craftily:

"Oh, don't be disturbed, Don Augusto, it was nothing at all! I beg your pardon. I had a sort of fit — I don't know what it was that I did — I was not conscious. And so, once more, thank you and thank you again! Thanks to you and thanks to — to her! Good-bye."

When he had gone, Augusto called Liduvina.

"Tell me, Liduvina, who was it that was just now here with me?"

"A young man."

"What did he look like?"

"But — do you need me to tell you that?"

"Honestly, was there somebody here with me?"

"Señorito!"

"No — no — swear to me that a young man was here with me, and then tell me what he looked like. Tall and blond, wasn't he? With a moustache, and stout rather than slender, and a Roman nose — tell me, was he here?"

"But aren't you feeling well, Don Augusto?"

"It wasn't a dream?"

"Not unless both of us were dreaming —— "

"No, we can't both dream the same dream at the same time. And that's the way we know it is

not a dream — when it is not one person's
alone —— "

"Well, then, don't worry any longer! Yes, the
person you are speaking of was here."

"And what did he say when he left?"

"He didn't speak to me when he left —
I didn't even see him —— "

"And do you know who he is, Liduvina?"

"Yes, I know him. He is the man who was the
lover of —— "

"That's enough. And now tell me, whose lover
is he now?"

"You are expecting me to know too much."

"But you women know so many things that
nobody teaches you —— "

"Yes, but to make up for that we can't seem
to learn what they want to teach us."

"Never mind about that, Liduvina. Now tell
me the truth: don't you really know who this —
this fellow is going with now?"

"No, but I can guess."

"How?"

"From what you tell me."

"Very well, and now call Domingo."

"What for?"

"I want to know whether I am not still dreaming, and whether you are really Liduvina or —— "

"Or whether Domingo is dreaming too? But
I think I know something better than that."

"What?"

"Call Orfeo."

"Good! He never dreams!"

A moment or two later, after Liduvina had left, the dog came into the room.

"Come here, Orfeo, come here!" said the master. "Poor little beggar! How short a time you have to live with me now! She doesn't want you in her house. But where shall I send you? What am I going to do with you? And what will become of you without me? For it may very well kill you, I am certain of that! It is only a dog that is capable of dying over the loss of his master. And I have been more to you than master. I have been your father, your God! She doesn't want you in the house, and she is going to drive you out. She doesn't want to see you by my side. Could it be that you, the very symbol of fidelity, would disturb the peace of her home? Who knows? Who knows whether a dog may not catch the most secret thoughts of the persons he lives with though he says nothing about it? And now I have to marry. There's no help for it, I must — otherwise I shall never wake from my dream. And wake I must.

"But why are you looking at me so, Orfeo? Really, you seem to be weeping without shedding tears! Is there something you want to say to me? I seem to see you suffering for lack of speech. How quick I was to say that you don't dream! Certainly you are dreaming now, Orfeo, and dreaming of me! Why is it that we men are men only because there are dogs and cats and horses and oxen and sheep and all kinds of animals, but especially because there are domestic animals? If there had been no domestic animals upon which to load the animality of life, would man ever have attained his humanity? If man had never domesticated the horse would not half of our race be now going through life with the other half on their backs? Yes, we owe our civilization to you. And to the women. But isn't woman only another domestic animal? And if they had no women would the men be men? Alas, Orfeo, there's one coming into the house who is going to drive you out!"

He pressed him to his breast, while the dog, who seemed really to be weeping, kept licking his chin.

XXIX

A L L was now ready for the wedding. Augusto wished it to be modest and quiet, but his future wife seemed to prefer celebrating it with more ostentation and éclat.

The nearer the day approached the more ardently Augusto longed to be permitted certain little liberties and intimacies. Eugenia, however, maintained a stricter reserve than ever.

"But, Eugenia, it's only a few days now before we shall belong to each other completely."

"Well, for that very reason. If we are to treat one another with respect it is necessary to begin now."

"Respect — respect — respect banishes affection."

"And so that is your idea of it! Man to the end!"

Meanwhile he noted that there was something strange and forced in her manner to him. At times it seemed that she was trying to avoid looking him in the face. And then he was reminded of his mother, and of her constant anxiety that her son should be happy in his marriage. And now too, just as he was about to be married to Eugenia, he found himself more than ever tormented by what Mauricio had said about carrying off Rosario. It made him jealous, madly jealous, to think of the opportunity he had allowed to pass and of the ridiculous picture of himself that he had left in the mind of the girl. "I dare say both of them are now laughing at me," he said to himself, "and he for a double reason; because in leaving Eugenia he has tied me up to her, and then because he has carried off Rosario." And at times he felt a mad desire to break his engagement, go off and make a conquest of Rosario, and snatch her away from Mauricio.

"And that chit, that Rosario, what has become of her?" Eugenia asked him a few days before the wedding.

"Why do you want to remind me of that now?"

"Oh, if the memory is unpleasant, I'll drop it."

"No, no, but —— "

"Yes, I remember how she interrupted us when I once called upon you. Have you ever heard anything more of her?" — and she gave him one of those glances that go straight through.

"No, I have never heard of her again."

"I wonder who can be making a conquest of her now — or who may now have won her —— "
And taking her eyes from Augusto, she let them

gaze into space, somewhere beyond the field of vision.

A host of strange omens passed through the mind of her lover. "She seems to know something," he said to himself; and then aloud:

"Do you happen to have heard anything about her?"

"I?" replied Eugenia, with an air of indifference, looking at him again.

The shadow of a mystery floated between them.

"I dare say that you have forgotten her —— "

"But what is the reason for your insistence upon talking about this — this girl?"

"Oh, I don't know —— Because — but, to change the subject, what does it mean to a man when another man gets possession of the woman he was after and carries her off?"

The blood rose surging to the head of Augusto as he heard this. He had a wild desire to rush out, run off in search of Rosario, win her, and bring her back to Eugenia, so as to say to Eugenia: "Here she is, and she belongs to me, and not to — *your* Mauricio!"

Three days remained before the day of the wedding. Augusto left his fiancée's house in a troubled state of mind. That night he could hardly sleep.

The following morning, just after waking, Liduvina entered his room.

"Here is a letter for the señorito. I think it is from the Señorita Eugenia —— "

"A letter? From her? A letter from her? Leave it here and go!"

Liduvina left the room. Augusto began to tremble. His heart was agitated by a strange uneasiness. He thought of Rosario, and then of Mauricio. But he was afraid to touch the letter. He gazed at the envelope with a kind of terror. He rose, washed, dressed, called for his breakfast, and bolted it down in a moment. "No," he said to himself, "I don't want to read it here." He left the house and went to the nearest church; and there, surrounded by a number of worshippers who were hearing mass, he opened the letter. "Here I shall be obliged to control myself," he said to himself, "for I don't know what it will be in my heart to do." The letter read:

"My esteemed Augusto: When you read these lines I shall be with Mauricio on his way to the place where he has been appointed to a position, thanks to your kindness. To your kindness I also owe the fact that I am able to enjoy the benefit of my rents; which, with his salary, will enable us to live together in some comfort. I do not ask you to forgive me. For after this you will surely be convinced that neither could I have made you happy nor, much less, you me. I shall write to you again after the first effect of this has passed, to explain why I am taking this step now, and in this fashion. Mauricio preferred that we should disappear on the wedding-day itself, after the wedding. But his plan was complicated; and besides, it seemed unnecessarily cruel to you. As I said to you on another occasion, I expect that we shall continue to be friends. Your friend,

Eugenia Domingo del Arco.
P. S. Rosario is not coming with us. She remains here, and you can console yourself with her."

Augusto dropped upon a bench, overcome. After a moment he knelt and prayed.

As he left the church it seemed to him that he was quite calm; but it was that terrible sultry calm that precedes the storm. He went to Eugenia's house and there he found the poor uncle and aunt in a state of dismay. The niece had failed to return home at night, and she had communicated her decision to them by letter. The pair had taken a train which left at nightfall, very shortly after Augusto's last conversation with his fiancée.

"What are we to do now?" said Doña Ermelinda.

"What are we to do, señora?" replied Augusto. "There's nothing to do but to accept the situation."

"This is an outrage," cried Don Fermín. "Things of this kind ought not to go unpunished — we ought to make an example of them!"

"What! You, Don Fermín? You, the anarchist?"

"What has that to do with it? Things of this kind are simply not done. To deceive a man in that fashion!"

"She didn't deceive the other man," said Augusto calmly; and after saying it he was terrified by the calmness with which he had said it.

"But she will deceive him — she will deceive him — you can count upon that!"

Augusto experienced a diabolical pleasure in the thought that in the end Eugenia would deceive Mauricio. "But not with me," he muttered to himself, in so low a tone that he hardly heard it himself.

"Well, señores — I am deeply grieved by what has taken place, and more than anything else because it concerns your niece. But now I must take leave of you."

"You understand, Don Augusto, that we ——" Doña Ermelinda began.

"Of course! I understand perfectly. But ——"

The visit was too painful to be prolonged further. After a few words more Augusto left.

As he walked along the street he was filled with terror of himself and of what was taking place in him — or rather, of what was not taking place in him. The coolness, on the surface at least, the utter calmness with which he had received this supreme stroke of mockery — this made him really doubtful of his own existence. "If I were a man like the others," he told himself, "a man with a heart — if I were even a man, if I really existed — how could I take this with the relative calmness with which I have taken it?" And unconsciously he began to pass his hands over his body and even to pinch himself to see if he felt anything.

Presently he felt something tugging at his trousers. It was Orfeo, who had run out to meet him and offer him consolation. At the sight of Orfeo he experienced, strange to say, great joy. He took him into his arms and said, "Congratulate yourself, little Orfeo, congratulate yourself! And let us congratulate one another! They won't drive you out of the house now; they won't take you away from me now; they won't part us now! Now we shall go on living together through life and death. There is no evil without its good, be the evil never so great, the good never so small — and no good without its evil. You, Orfeo, you are faithful; you are the faithful one! I dare say that some day you'll be looking for your mate; but not for that

will you leave the house, not for that will you abandon your master. You are faithful! And I say, I'll
bring a bitch to live in the house, so that you will
not have to leave me. Yes, I'll go and fetch her.
For I wonder — did you run out to meet me with
the idea of consoling me for the pain that I must
be suffering, or was it that you happened to meet
me on your way home from a visit to your lady-
love? In any case, you are faithful, you are the
faithful one. And now nobody is going to throw
you out of my house; nobody will part us."

He entered the house. Hardly had he found
himself home again and alone when the tempest in
his soul, which had seemed so calm, was unchained.
A flood of emotion swept through him in which
were mingled sadness, bitter sadness, jealousy, rage,
fear, hate, pity, contempt, and above all else shame
— an overwhelming shame, a terrible consciousness
of the ridicule and contempt that were clinging
to him.

"She has been the death of me!" he said to
Liduvina.

"Who?"

"She."

He shut himself up in his room. By the side
of the pictures of Eugenia and Mauricio, floating
before his mind, appeared the image of Rosario,
also mocking him. He thought of his mother. He
threw himself upon the bed and stuffed the pillow

between his teeth. There was nothing he could say to himself, he could not form a single clear idea. His monologue had gone mute. He felt as if his soul had withered. He burst into tears. He wept and wept and wept; and in the silent weeping his thought was gradually dissolved.

xxx

V ICTOR found Augusto, who had collapsed in a corner of the sofa, looking down at the floor and through it.

"What's the matter?" he asked, putting a hand on Augusto's shoulder.

"You ask me what is the matter? Don't you know what has happened to me?"

"Yes, I know what has happened to you externally; which means that I know what she has done to you. What I don't know is what is going on inside of you. In other words, I don't know why you are taking it in this fashion."

"The whole thing seems incredible!"

"But granting that one love has slipped away from you — love *a*, let us call it — haven't you still got *b*, or *c*, or *x*, or any other of the *n?*"

"It seems to me this is no time for jesting."

"On the contrary, this is just the time for jesting."

"What hurts me most is not the lost love. It's the ridicule! the scorn! the mockery! the mockery! They have mocked at me and made a laughing-stock of me! They have made me out ridiculous

and contemptible! They wanted to demonstrate —
I don't know what — that I do not exist."

"What luck!"

"Don't joke about it, Victor."

"But why shouldn't I joke about it? You set
out to make an experiment and they have made
you the experiment. You wanted to make her the
frog and she has made you the frog. Jump into the
pool, then, and croak for your living!"

"I ask you again —— "

"Not to jest, eh? Well, I am going to jest.
Jests were made for such occasions as this."

"But yours are corrosive."

"Ah, but it is necessary to corrode. And to
confound. Above all else, to confound; and to confound everything. Dream with waking, fiction
with reality, the true with the false; to confound
them all in one homogeneous mist. A jest that is not
corrosive and confounding is of no use whatever.
In tragedy the child smiles, in comedy the old man
weeps. You wanted to make her the frog, she has
made a frog of you. Accept the situation, then,
and make a frog of yourself."

"What do you mean by that?"

"Experiment upon yourself."

"Yes, kill myself, you mean."

"I am not saying either yes or no to that. It
would be one solution among others, but not the
best."

"Then hunt them up and kill them?"

"To kill for the sake of killing is an absurdity. It's good at best for purging yourself of hate, which is corrupting to the soul. More than one bitter soul has cured himself of his bitterness, and then found himself with a feeling of pity and even of love for his victim, once he had satisfied his hatred upon him. The evil act frees us from the evil passion. And this is because law makes sin."

"But what am I going to do?"

"You must have heard that in this world one must either devour or be devoured —— "

"Yes, make a laughing-stock of others or have them make a laughing-stock of you."

"No, there's a third possibility, which is to devour yourself, make a laughing-stock of yourself. Devour yourself, then! He who devours, enjoys; but he is not satisfied by reflecting upon the end of his enjoyment, and he becomes a pessimist. He who is being devoured suffers; but he is not satisfied to wait for his release from pain, and he becomes an optimist. Devour yourself, then; and since the pleasure of devouring and the pain of being devoured will be confounded, each will neutralize the other, and you will arrive at that spiritual state of perfect equanimity which is called ataraxy. Then you will be merely a spectacle for yourself."

"And it is you; you, Victor, who come to me with this kind of thing?"

"Yes, it is I, Augusto, it is I."

"Well, there was a time when you didn't think in this — this corrosive fashion."

"Then I was not a parent."

"And being a parent — does that?"

"Being a parent? To those who are neither madmen nor fools being a parent brings the most terrible awakening in a man's life: the sense of responsibility! To meditate upon the mystery of paternity is enough to drive one mad. And if most parents do not go mad, it is because most parents are stupid — or they are not really parents. Rejoice, then, Augusto, and remember that in losing your love you have escaped the danger of becoming a parent. When I advised you to marry I did not advise you to become a parent. Matrimony is an experiment — a psychological experiment; paternity is also an experiment, but — pathological."

"But she has made me a parent, Victor!"

"Made you a parent? How?"

"Yes, my own parent! In this experience I seem for the first time to have been really born. And born to suffer — to die."

"Yes, the second birth, the real birth, consists in being born through pain to that consciousness of ever-continuing death of which we are dying all through life. But if you have become your own parent, that means that you have also become your own child."

"It seems all incredible! Incredible, Victor,
that after what has happened and after what has
been done to me by — by her, that after that I
should still be able to listen quietly to these subtleties of yours, this conceptual legerdemain, these
macabresque jests — and what is worse —— "

"What?"

"That they should divert me. It makes me
furious with myself."

"All of that belongs to the comedy, Augusto.
The comedy that we perform before ourselves,
in what is called the inner forum, on the stage of
our inner consciousness, playing at the same time
the part of actor and of spectator. It gives one a
rasping sense of discord to discover that when the
scene presented is a scene of pain one has a sudden
desire to laugh. But that is just when the impulse
to laugh is strongest. Ah, comedy! The comedy of
pain!"

"And suppose the comedy of pain drives one
to suicide?"

"Then the comedy of suicide!"

"But the suicide is real!"

"Comedy, just the same!"

"Then tell me, is anything ever real or true?
Is there anything that we ever really sense?"

"But who told you that comedy was not real
or true or that in comedy nothing is really sensed?"

"Well — and what do you make of it, then?"

"That all things are one and the same; that things have to be confounded, Augusto, confounded. And he who refuses to confound them confounds himself."

"And he who confounds them also confounds himself."

"Perhaps."

"But what then?"

"Why, this: all this dialectical subtlety and talk, this juggling with words and definitions — it serves to pass the time!"

"Those who indulge in it are certainly passing the time!"

"And you too! Have you ever found yourself of such absorbing interest in your own eyes as you are now? How is a man to know that he has limbs if they don't pain him?"

"Very good; but tell me what I am going to do."

"Do — do — do! Bah! You seem to have the idea now that you are the hero of a play or a novel! For ourselves, let us be content with being characters in a — *nivola!* Do — do — do! Do you think we are doing little in spending the time here talking? It's the mania for action — in other words, for pantomime! When you hear that a drama is full of action it means that the actors are indulging in a host of gestures, performing mighty deeds, fighting stage duels, skipping about and — pantomime! pantomime! Or you may hear that there is too much talk in the play. As if talk were not action! In the beginning was the Word, and by the Word all things were made. Suppose, for example, that some — some 'nivolist' were hiding here now, back of that wardrobe, and taking stenographic notes of all that we are saying — suppose that he should reproduce them, very likely his readers would say that there is nothing happening here; and yet —— "

"Ah, Victor, they wouldn't say that if they could see inside!"

"Inside? Inside whom? You? Me? We haven't any inside. The time when they would not say that nothing is happening here, would be when they could see the inside of themselves — of themselves, the readers. The soul of a character in a play, in a novel, or in a *nivola,* has no inside except that of the —— "

"Yes, of the author."

"No, of the reader."

"Well, I can assure you, Victor —— "

"Don't assure me of anything. Devour yourself. That is the surest thing."

"But I am already devouring myself, Victor; that is just what I am doing. I began, Victor, by being a kind of shadow, a fiction. For years I have wandered about like a spectre, like a manikin formed out of mist, not believing in my own existence, imagining myself to be a sort of fanciful character which some hidden genius had created for his own consolation or relief. But now, after what has happened, after what they have done to me, after this mockery, this cruelty of jest — now, now I do feel my own existence, now I can actually touch myself. Now I no longer doubt that I am real!"

"Comedy! Comedy! Comedy!"

"How?"

"Yes, it's part of the comedy that he who plays the part of king thinks that he really is king."

But what are you getting at in all this? What is your object?"

"I want to distract you. And besides, supposing that, as I suggested, there is a 'nivolist' here in hiding who is listening to us and taking down our words for the purpose of reproducing them — well, I want to make the reader of his *nivola* doubtful of his own solid reality, if only for a passing moment, and take his turn in believing that he is only a 'nivolistic' personage like ourselves."

"But what for?"

"For his salvation."

"Yes, I have heard someone say that the most liberating effect of art is that it makes one forget that one exists. There are people who plunge into novel-reading only to take their attention off themselves and forget their troubles —— "

"No, the most liberating effect of art is that it makes one doubt whether one does exist."

"But what is it to exist?"

"There! Do you see now? Now you are beginning to recover; you are beginning now to devour yourself. 'To be or not to be! —' thus said Hamlet, one of those who invented Shakespeare."

"Well, for my own part, Victor, this 'to be or not to be' has always seemed to me a piece of solemn nonsense."

"The more profound a saying the emptier it always is. The greatest profundity of all is that of a well without a bottom. Tell me this: what would you say to be the truest of all truths?"

"Why — let me think — that statement of Descartes: 'I think, therefore I am.'"

"No, it's only: $A = A$."

"But that doesn't mean anything!"

"And that is just why it is the truest of all truths — because there's nothing in it. But as for that Cartesian nonsense, do you think that it is really so incontrovertible?"

"And so! ——"

"Very well. Did Descartes say it?"

"Yes, of course!"

"Then it wasn't true. For since Descartes was never anything but a fictitious entity himself, being an invention of history, why — he neither existed nor did he think!"

"Who is your authority for that?"

"No authority; the thing is self-evident."

"Do you mean, then, that he who was, and who thought, was simply thought itself?"

"Precisely. And then remember that this is the equivalent of saying that to be is to think, and that that which does not think cannot be."

"Of course!"

"Then don't think, Augusto, don't think. But if you insist upon thinking —— "

"Well?"

"Devour yourself!"

"In other words, commit suicide —— ?"

"I'll have nothing to do with that. Good-bye."

Victor departed, leaving Augusto alone with his reflections, lost and confounded.

XXXI

*T*HE storm in the soul of Augusto ended in a terrible calm: he had resolved to kill himself. He wanted to put an end to that self which had been the cause of all his misery. But before carrying out his plan it occurred to him, like a drowning sailor who grasps at a straw, to come and talk it over with me, the author of this whole story. Augusto had read an essay of mine in which I made a passing reference to suicide and this, together with some other things of mine that he had read, had evidently made such an impression upon him that he did not wish to leave this world without having met me and talked with me for a while. Accordingly, he came here to Salamanca, where I have been living for twenty years past, to pay me a visit.

When his call was announced I smiled enigmatically, and I had him come into my study. He entered like a ghost. He looked at a portrait of me in oil which presides over the books of my library, and then at a sign from me he took a seat opposite me.

He began by speaking of my literary works, in particular of those that were more or less philosophical, showing that he knew them very well; which, of course, did not fail to please me. Then he began to tell me of his life and of his misfortunes. I interrupted him by telling him to spare himself the trouble; I was as familiar with the vicissitudes of his life as he himself; and this I demonstrated to him by citing some of the most intimate details, and in particular some things that he thought to be utterly hidden. He looked at me with genuine terror in his eyes, as one looks at some incredible being. I seemed to see a change in the colour and in the lines of his face, and I saw that he even trembled. I had him fascinated.

"It hardly seems true," he kept repeating, "it hardly seems true. I shouldn't believe it if I had not seen it. I don't know whether I am awake or dreaming —— "

"Neither awake nor dreaming," I replied.

"I can't explain it — I can't explain it," he went on. "But since you seem to know as much about me as I know myself, perhaps you guess my purpose in coming."

"Yes," I said. "You" — and I gave to this "you" the emphasis of authority — "you, oppressed by the weight of your misfortunes, have conceived the diabolical idea of killing yourself; and before doing it, impelled by something you have read in one of my last essays, you have come to consult me about it."

The poor man shook like a drop of mercury and looked at me with the stare of one possessed. He tried to rise, perhaps with the idea of flight, but he could not. He could not summon the strength.

"No, don't move," I commanded him.

"Do you mean — do you mean —— " he stammered.

"I mean that you cannot commit suicide even if you wish to do so."

"What!" he cried, finding himself so flatly opposed and contradicted.

"Yes, if a man is going to kill himself what is the first thing that is necessary?" I asked him.

"That he should have the courage to do it," he replied.

"No," I said, "that he should be alive."

"Of course!"

"And you are not alive."

"Not alive! What do you mean? Do you mean that I have died?" And without clearly knowing what he was doing he began to pass his hands over his body.

"No, my man, no!" I replied. "I told you before that you were neither waking nor sleeping; now I tell you that you are neither alive nor dead."

"Tell me all of it at once; God, tell me all," he begged me in terror. "With what I am seeing and hearing this afternoon I am afraid of going mad."

"Very well, then. The truth is, my dear Augusto," I spoke to him the softest of tones, "you can't kill yourself because you are not alive; and you are not alive — or dead either — because you do not exist."

"I don't exist! What do you mean by that?"

"No, you do not exist except as a fictitious entity, a character of fiction. My poor Augusto, you are only a product of my imagination and of the imagination of those of my readers who read this story which I have written of your fictitious adventures and misfortunes. You are nothing more than a personage in a novel, or a *nivola,* or whatever you choose to call it. Now, then, you know your secret."

Upon hearing this the poor man continued to look at me for a while with one of those perforating looks that seem to pierce your own gaze and go beyond; presently he glanced for a moment at the portrait in oil which presides over my books, then his colour returned and his breathing became easier, and gradually recovering, he was again master of himself. He rested his elbows on the arm of the sofa opposite me, against which he was leaning; and then with his face in the palms of his hands he looked at me with a smile and he said slowly:

"Listen to me, Don Miguel — it can't be that you are mistaken, and that what is happening is precisely the contrary of what you think and of what you have told me?"

"And what do you mean by the contrary?" I asked, rather alarmed to see him regaining his self-possession.

"May it not be, my dear Don Miguel," he continued, "that it is you and not I who are the fictitious entity, the one that does not really exist, who is neither living nor dead? May it not be that you are nothing more than a pretext for bringing my history into the world?"

"Really this is too much!" I cried, now becoming irritated.

"Please don't get so excited, Señor de Unamuno," he replied. "Keep calm. You have expressed doubts about my existence ——— "

"Doubts? No!" I interrupted. "Absolute certainty that you do not exist outside of the novel that I have created."

"Very well; then please don't be disturbed if I in turn doubt your existence rather than my own. Let us come to the point. Are you not the person who has said, not once but several times, that Don Quixote and Sancho are not only real persons but more real than Cervantes himself?"

"I can't deny it, but the sense in which I said it was ——— "

"Very well, never mind in what sense. Let us come to another point. When a man who is lying asleep in his bed dreams of something, which is it that more truly exists, he as the consciousness that dreams or the dreams themselves?"

"And what if the dreamer dreams that he himself exists?" — I turned the question on him.

"In that case, friend Don Miguel, my own question would be, in what fashion does he exist? As the dreamer who dreams of himself or as something dreamed by himself? And note this, moreover: in entering this discussion with me you are already recognizing me as an existence independent of yourself."

"Not at all. No, not at all," I said quickly. "In entering this discussion I am merely satisfying a private need of my own. Apart from discussion and contradiction I am never alive; and when there is no one outside of me to question and contradict me I invent some one to do it within me. My monologues are dialogues."

"And perhaps the dialogues that you fabricate are nothing more than monologues."

"It may be. But in any case I tell you, and I wish to repeat it, that you do not exist outside of me ———— "

"And I will again suggest this to you, namely, that you do not exist outside of me and of the other characters that you think you have invented. I am certain that Don Avito Carrascal would be of my opinion and the great Don Fulgencio —— "

"You needn't mention them —— "

"Very well, then, I won't; but you shouldn't make fun of them. And now let us see; what do you really think about my suicide?"

"I think, then, that since you do not exist except in my imagination — as I tell you again — and since you neither ought nor are you able to do anything but just what I please, and since it does not really suit me that you should kill yourself — well, you are not going to kill yourself. And that settles it."

"Your saying that 'it does not really suit me' is very Spanish, Señor de Unamuno, but it is far from edifying. Moreover, even granting your strange theory that I do not really exist and that you do, that I am nothing but a character of fiction, the product of your imagination as a novelist — or as a 'nivolist' — even so there is no reason why I should submit to 'what really suits you,' that is, to your caprice. For even those whom we call characters of fiction have their own inwrought logic —— "

"Yes, I know that song."

"But, really, it is a fact that neither a novelist nor a playwright is at all able to do anything that happens to occur to him, to a character that he creates. That a fictitious character in a novel should do that which no reader would ever expect him to do, is forbidden by all of the established principles of art —— "

"Doubtless a character in a novel —— "

"Well, then?"

"But a character in a *nivola* — a 'nivolistic' character —— "

"Let us drop these buffooneries. They are offensive, and they wound me where I am most sensitive. Whether of myself, as I think, or because you have given it to me, as you suppose, I have my own character, my own manner of being, my own inwrought logic, and this logic demands that I kill myself —— "

"You may think so, but you are wrong."

"Let us see. Why am I wrong? And where am I wrong? Show me where my mistake lies. Since the most difficult knowledge that there is, is knowing yourself, I may easily be mistaken and it may be that suicide is not the logical solution of my problem. But prove it to me. For though this self-knowledge be difficult, Don Miguel, there is another kind of knowledge that seems no less difficult —— "

"And that is? —— " I asked.

He looked at me with a smile that was shrewd and enigmatic and then he said slowly:

"Well, that which is more difficult than self-knowledge is this: that a novelist or a playwright should know the characters that he creates or thinks he creates."

These sallies of Augusto were beginning to make me uneasy and I was losing my patience.

"And I insist," he added, "that even granting you have given me my being — a fictitious being, if you please — even so, and because it is so, you cannot prevent me from killing myself just because, as you say, it does not really suit you."

"Very well, that will do — enough!" I cried, bringing my fist down on the sofa, "Hold your tongue! I don't wish to hear any more impertinence! And from a creature of mine, too! And since I have had enough of you and I don't know, moreover, what more to do with you, I have now decided, not that you may not now kill yourself, but that I shall kill you. You are to die, then, but soon! Very soon!"

Augusto was horror-struck. "What!" he cried. "Do you mean that you are going to let me die, make me die — you are going to kill me?"

"Yes, I am going to cause you to die."

"Oh, never! never! never!" he shrieked.

"Ah!" I said, looking at him with mingled pity and rage. "And so you were ready to kill yourself, but you don't want me to kill you? And you were about to take your own life, but you object to my taking it?"

"Yes, it is not the same thing ——"

"To be sure, it is not. I have heard of cases of that kind. I heard of a man who went out one night armed with a revolver, intending to take his own life, when some thieves undertook to rob him. They attacked him, he defended himself, killed one of them and the others fled. And then, seeing that he had bought his life at the cost of another's, he renounced his intention."

"One can understand that," observed Augusto. "It was a matter of taking the life of somebody, of killing a man; and after he had killed another, what was the use of killing himself? Most suicides are frustrated homicides; men kill themselves because they have not the courage to kill others —— "

"Ah! now I understand you, Augusto, I understand. You mean that if you had had the courage to kill Eugenia or Mauricio, or both, you would not be thinking of killing yourself, isn't that so?"

"Let me tell you, it is not precisely of them that I am thinking — no!"

"Of whom, then?"

"Of you" — and he looked me straight in the eye.

"What!" I cried, rising to my feet. "What! Have you conceived the idea of killing me? You? And of killing me?"

"Sit down and keep cool. Do you think, Don Miguel, that it would be the first case in which a

fictitious entity, as you call me, had killed him
whom he believed to have given him his being —
his fictitious being, of course?"

"This is really too much," I said, walking up
and down my study. "This passes all limits. This
couldn't happen except —— "

"Except in *nivolas*," Augusto completed with
a drawl.

"Very well, enough! enough! enough! This is
more than I can stand. You came here to consult
me — me, you understand — and you? You begin
by disputing my own existence, forgetting that I
have the right to do with you anything that suits
me — yes, just what I say, anything that may happen to occur to —— "

"Don't be so Spanish, Don Miguel —— "

"And now this too, you idiot! Well, yes, I am
indeed a Spaniard, Spanish by birth, by education,
Spanish in mind, body, and language and almost
by profession and occupation; Spanish above everything and before everything. Spanishism is my religion, the heaven in which I wish to believe is a
celestial and eternal Spain, and my God is a Spanish God, the God of our Lord Don Quixote, a God
who thinks in Spanish and who said in Spanish, Let
there be light! *Sea luz!* — his word was a Spanish
word —— "

"Well, and what of it?" he interrupted, re-
calling me to reality.

"And now you have conceived the idea of killing me. Of killing me — *me?* And you? Am I to die at the hands of one of my creatures? I'll stand no more of it. And so to punish you for your insolence, and to put an end to these disintegrating, extravagant, and anarchistic ideas with which you have come to me, I hereby render judgment and pass the sentence that you are to die. As soon as you reach home you shall die. You shall die, I tell you, you shall die."

"But — for God's sake!" cried Augusto, now in a tone of supplication, pale and trembling with fear.

"There is no God that can help you. You shall die."

"Yes, but I want to live, Don Miguel, I want to live — I want to live —— "

"Weren't you just now thinking of killing yourself?"

"Oh! if that is why, Don Miguel, then I swear to you that I will not kill myself, I will not take away this life which God, or yourself, has given me; I swear it to you — now that you wish to kill me I myself want to live — to live — to live —— "

"What a life!" I exclaimed.

"Yes, whatever it may be. I want to live even though I am again to be mocked at, even though another Eugenia and another Mauricio tear my heart out. I wish to live — live — live —— "

"Now it cannot be — it cannot be —— "

"I want to live — live — I want to be myself, myself, myself."

"But what if that self is only what I wish you to be —— ?"

"I wish to be myself — to be myself! I wish to live!" and his voice was choked with sobs.

"It cannot be — cannot be —— "

"Listen, Don Miguel, for the sake of your children, of your wife, of whatever is dearest to you! Remember that you will then cease to be yourself — that *you* will die —— "

He fell on his knees at my feet, begging and imploring me: "Don Miguel, for God's sake! I want to live. I want to be myself."

"It cannot be, my poor Augusto," I said, taking him by the hand and lifting him up. "It cannot be. I have now decreed it — it is written — and irrevocably; you can live no longer. I no longer know what to do with you. God, when he does not know what to do with us, kills us. And I do not forget that there passed through your mind the idea of killing me —— "

"But, Don Miguel, if I —— "

"It makes no difference. I know where I stand. And really I am afraid that if I do not kill you soon, you will end by killing me."

"But are we not agreed that —— ?"

"It cannot be, Augusto, it cannot be. Your

hour has come. It is now written, and I cannot now recall it. And for all that your life can now be worth to you —— "

"But — good God!"

"There is neither 'but' nor 'God' that can avail you. Go!"

"And so you won't?" he said. "You refuse? You are unwilling to let me be myself, come out of the mist and live, live, live; to see myself, hear myself, touch myself, feel myself, feel my own pain, be myself — you are unwilling, then? And so I am to die as a fictitious character? Very well, then, my lord creator Don Miguel, you too are to die, you too! And you will return to that nothing from which you came! God will cease to dream you! You are to die, yes, you are to die, even though you do not wish to; and die shall all of those who read my story, all of them, all, all, without a single exception. Fictitious entities like myself — just like myself! All of them are to die; all, all. And it is I who tell you this — I, Augusto Pérez, a fictitious entity, a 'nivolistic' entity, just like yourself. For as for you, my creator Don Miguel, you too are only a 'nivolistic' entity, and your readers are 'nivolistic' entities, just like me, just the same as Augusto Pérez, your victim —— "

"Victim!" I cried.

"Victim, yes! To create me only to let me die! Well, you too are to die! He who creates cre-

ates himself, and he who creates himself dies. You
will die, Don Miguel, you will die, and all those
who think me, they are to die too! To death,
then!"

This supreme effort of the passion for life —
of the thirst for immortality — left poor Augusto
utterly weak.

I pushed him towards the door. He walked
out with his eyes fixed upon the ground, passing his
hands wonderingly over himself as if he were uncertain of his own existence. I wiped away a furtive tear.

XXXII

T H A T same night Augusto left this
city of Salamanca, whither he had come to pay
me a visit. He left with the sentence of death resting upon his soul and with the conviction that it
would be practically impossible for him to commit
suicide even though he tried to do so. Having in
mind my sentence of death, the poor boy endeav-
oured to prolong as much as possible the journey
to his home, but a mysterious attraction, an inner
force, drew him towards it. It was a pitiable journey. Riding along in the train he counted the minutes, counted them literally: one, two, three, four.
His misfortunes, the sad dream of his love affairs
with Eugenia and Rosario, the tragicomic history
of his vain attempts at marriage — all this had been
blotted from his memory, or rather had been dissolved into mist. He hardly felt the contact of the
seat upon which he rested or the weight of his
body. "Can it be true that I do not really exist?"
he kept saying to himself. "Can it be that this man
is right in saying that I am only a product of his
fancy, purely a character of fiction?"

Sad and painful in the extreme had been his
life of late, but for him it was far sadder, for him
it was far more painful to reflect that in the end
it had been nothing but a dream, and not his own
dream, but mine. To be nothing at all seemed to
him more dreadful than to live and suffer. To
dream that one lives, and only to dream it — that
perhaps might be endured, but to be only the
dream of another! ——

"And why should it be that I do not exist?"
he said to himself. "Why? Suppose it be true. that
this man has imagined me, dreamed me, created
me in his imagination; do I not still live in the imagination of others, of those at any rate who read
this story of my life? And if in this fashion I live
in the fancy of several persons — well, isn't that
perhaps just what is real, that which is found in
several minds and not merely in one? And why may
I not, then, rising from the pages of the book in
which the story of my life is stored, or rather from
the minds of those who read it — of you who are
now reading it — why may I not exist in the form
of an eternal and of an eternally sad soul? Why
not?"

The poor fellow could get no rest. The plains
of Castile passed before his sight, covered now with
oaks and now with pines; his eyes rested upon the
snowy peaks of the sierras; and looking back, behind him, all enveloped in mist, at the faces of the

men and women who had been his companions in life, he felt himself carried along to his death.

He reached his house and rang, and Liduvina, who opened the door, turned pale at the sight of him.

"What's the matter, Liduvina? What are you alarmed at?"

"Jesus! Jesus! The señorito looks more dead than alive. He has the face of somebody from another world."

"I come from another world, Liduvina, and I am going to another world. And I am neither dead nor alive."

"But — has he gone mad? Domingo! Domingo!"

"Don't call your husband, Liduvina. I am not mad. No! Nor, as I said before, am I dead, though I shall die very soon; nor am I alive either."

"But — what in the world are you saying?"

"That I do not exist, Liduvina, that I do not exist; that I am a fictitious entity like a character in a novel."

"Bah! stuff out of books! Take something strengthening. Get your clothes off and go to bed and pay no attention to these fancies."

"But, Liduvina, do you believe that I do not exist?"

"Come, come! drop this game, señorito; have some supper and go to bed! And tomorrow will be another day!"

"I think, therefore I am," said Augusto to himself; and then he added: "Everything that thinks is, and everything that is thinks. Yes, everything that is thinks. I am, therefore I think."

At first he felt no appetite for supper, and it was only as a matter of habit and for the sake of yielding to the entreaties of his faithful servants that he asked them to serve him a couple of boiled eggs and nothing more, a mere trifle. But as he proceeded to eat a strange appetite developed within him, a rage for eating more and more. He called for two more eggs, and afterwards for a beefsteak.

"Good! Good!" said Liduvina, "go on and eat. Very likely this is only an attack of weakness. He who doesn't eat dies."

"And he who eats dies also, Liduvina," observed Augusto sadly.

"Yes, but not of hunger."

"And what difference does it make whether he dies of hunger or of anything else?"

And presently he thought: "But no! No! It can't be that I am to die. Only he can die who is alive, who exists; and since I do not exist I cannot die — I am immortal. There is no such immortality as that of one who, like myself, has never been born and does not exist. A character of fiction is an idea, and an idea is always immortal ——

"I am immortal! I am immortal!" cried Augusto.

"What did you say?" asked Liduvina as she hastened into the room.

"You may bring me — let me see — some jellied ham, some cold meat, *foie gras,* anything that you have. I am getting a voracious appetite."

"I am glad to see it so, señorito. Go on and eat! For a man who has an appetite is a man in good health, and the man who is in good health lives."

"But, Liduvina, I am not living."

"What is that you say?"

"Of course I am not living. We immortals do not live, and I am not living. I more than live — I live on. I am an idea, an idea!"

He began to devour the ham. "But if I eat," he said to himself, "how can it be that I am not alive? I eat, therefore I exist. There is no doubt whatever. *Edo, ergo sum.* What can be the cause of this voracious appetite?" And then he remembered having read several times that those who are condemned to death give themselves up to eating in the last hours, which they pass in the chapel. "It is a thing that I have never been able to account for," he said to himself. "The other kind of thing that Renan relates in his *L'Abbesse de Jouarre* is in-

telligible. It is quite intelligible that a couple condemned to death should feel just before dying the
instinct to survive by reproducing themselves. But
to eat! And yet — yes, yes, it is doubtless the body
defending itself. The soul when it learns that it
is to die becomes saddened or exalted, but the body,
if it is a sound body, develops a furious appetite.
For the body also knows. Yes, it is my body defending itself. I eat voraciously, therefore I am
about to die."

"Liduvina, bring me some cheese and cakes —
and fruit."

"But this seems to me overmuch, señorito; it is
too much. You'll hurt yourself."

"But wasn't it you who said that he who eats
lives?"

"Yes, but not in this fashion, not as you are
eating now —— My señorito must have heard the
saying, 'Food killed more than Avicena cured.' "

"Food can't kill *me*."

"Why not?"

"Because I am not alive, I do not exist. I have
already told you that."

Liduvina went to call her husband. "Domingo," she said, "it seems to me that the señorito
has gone mad. He says such very strange things —
things out of books — that he does not exist — and
I don't know what."

"What is wrong, señorito?" said Domingo,

coming into the room. "What has happened to you?"

"Oh, Domingo!" replied Augusto in the far-away tone of a ghost. "I can't help it, but I have a mad dread of going to bed."

"Then don't go to bed."

"No, no, I must; I can't stand on my feet."

"I think that the señorito ought to walk off the effects of his supper. He has eaten too much."

Augusto made an effort to rise to his feet.

"Don't you see, Domingo, don't you see? I can't stand on my feet."

"Of course, with your stomach stuffed so full."

"On the contrary, a little ballast helps a man keep his feet. The fact is, I do not exist. Let me tell you: a little while ago while I was having supper it seemed as if all that I ate fell from my mouth into a bottomless cask. He who eats lives, Liduvina is right; but he who eats as I have eaten tonight — driven by despair — is he who does not exist. I do not exist."

"Come, come! stop this nonsense! Take your coffee and your liqueur to settle your dinner and let us take a walk. I'll go with you."

"No, I can't stand on my feet. Don't you see?"

"Yes, that's right."

"Come here and let me lean on you. I want

you to sleep in my room tonight. We'll lay a mat-
tress on the floor for you, and you can watch over
me."

"It would be better for me not to lie down at
all, señorito, but to stay right here in an armchair —— "

"No, no, I want you to go to bed and sleep.
I want to feel you asleep, or rather to hear you
snore."

"Just as you wish."

"And now, look here, bring me a sheet of
paper. I am going to write out a telegram which
you are to send to its destination as soon as I am
dead —— "

"But — señorito!"

"Do what I tell you!"

Domingo obeyed; he brought the paper and
the inkstand, and August wrote:

"Salamanca
            Unamuno
You have had your own way. I am dead.
                        Augusto Pérez."

"You'll send this as soon as I am dead, won't
you?"

"Just as you wish," replied the servant, not
wishing to argue with his master.

The two went into the bedroom. Poor Augusto was trembling so violently that when he tried

to undress he could not get hold of his clothes to take them off.

"You undress me!" he said to Domingo.

"But what is the matter with you, señorito? Really, you look as if you had had a vision of the devil! You are as cold and white as snow. Do you wish me to call a doctor?"

"No, no, it is of no use."

"We'll warm the bed for you."

"What for? Leave it alone. And undress me completely, completely. Leave me as my mother brought me into the world, as I was born — if indeed I was ever born!"

"Don't say things like that, señorito!"

"Lay me down now. I want you yourself to lay me on the bed, for I can't move."

Poor Domingo, now thoroughly terrified, put his master to bed.

"And now, Domingo, I want you to be repeating in my ear, slowly, the *Pater Noster*, the *Ave Maria* and the *Salve*. That's the way — a little at a time" — and, after he had repeated them to himself: "Now listen, take hold of my right hand and pull at it. It does not seem to be mine, just as if I had lost it — and help me to make the sign of the cross — that's the way. This arm must be dead —— See if my pulse is beating —— Now leave me; leave me and let me see if I can sleep a little — but cover me up, cover me well."

"Yes, it is better for you to sleep," said Domingo as he tucked the blankets in around him.
"This will pass off if you sleep."

"Yes, it will pass off if I sleep —— But tell
me, tell me if I have ever done anything else but
sleep? Anything but dream? Has the whole thing
been anything but mist?"

"Come! Come! Don't say things like that. All
of that is just stuff out of books, as my Liduvina
says."

"Stuff out of books — stuff out of books —
and what is there, Domingo, that is not stuff out of
books? Can you say that before there were books,
in some form or other, before there were stories,
or words, before there was thought — there was
anything whatever? And after thought has ceased
will anything remain? Stuff out of books! Who is
not stuff out of books? Domingo, do you know
Don Miguel de Unamuno?"

"Yes, I have read something about him in
the papers. They say that he is a rather strange
man who makes a business of speaking truths that
have nothing to do with the case —— "

"But do you know him?"

"I? But why do you ask?"

"Because Unamuno is also stuff out of books
— all of us are! And he will die, he'll die too, even
though he doesn't want to, he will die. And that
will be my vengeance. He is not willing to let me

live? Very well, then he will die too, he will die, die."

"Very good. Let this señor rest in peace and die when God wills it, and you yourself go to sleep!"

"To sleep — to sleep — to dream —— To die — to sleep — to sleep — perchance to dream — I think, therefore I am; I am, therefore I think. I do not exist, no! I do not exist —— Oh, Mother dear! Eugenia — Rosario — Unamuno —— " And he fell asleep.

A few moments later he sat up in bed, livid, gasping, his eyes black and ghastly, seeking to penetrate the darkness, and shrieking: "Eugenia! Eugenia!" Domingo hastened to his side. His head dropped upon his breast and he was dead.

When the doctor arrived he thought at first that Augusto was still alive, and considered bleeding him and applying plasters; but very soon the sad fact was clear to him.

"It was some trouble with the heart — an asystolism," said the doctor.

"No, señor," replied Domingo. "It was indigestion. He ate tremendously, as he was not used to doing, in a way he had outgrown, just as if he intended —— "

"Yes, to make up for what he was not going to eat in the future, isn't that what you mean? Perhaps his heart gave him a presentiment of death."

"But in my opinion it was his head," said Liduvina. "Of course he ate an outlandish amount of supper, but as if he hardly knew what he was doing, and all the time saying crazy things —— "

"What kind of crazy things?" asked the doctor.

"That he did not exist, and things of that kind."

"Crazy things?" the physician went on saying under his breath, as if speaking to himself. "Who knows whether he did exist or not? Certainly not he himself — it is the man himself who knows least about his own existence. Each of us exists only for others." And then, he added, speaking aloud:

"The heart, the stomach, and the head — these three are one and the same thing."

"Yes, they are all parts of the body," said Domingo.

"And the body is one and the same single thing."

"Without doubt!"

"But more than enters your head."

"And you know, señor, how much enters my head?"

"Well, I know this: I can see that you are not stupid."

"I don't take myself for stupid, Señor Medico, and I don't understand those people who seem to think that every person they meet is a fool if they can't prove that he isn't."

"Very good — But as I was saying," continued the doctor, "the stomach works up the fluids that form the blood, the heart uses them to flood the head and the stomach, so that they may do their work, and the head controls the movements of the stomach and of the heart. And therefore this Señor Don Augusto has died in all three; he has died in his whole body — by synthesis."

"But it is my opinion," interposed Liduvina, "that in the case of my señorito someone put it into his head to die; and of course if a man is set upon dying, in the end he dies."

"Of course!" said the doctor. "If a man did not believe he was going to die, very likely he would not die, even though he were then in the very agony of death. But as soon as he has the slightest suspicion that he is bound to die, he is lost."

"In the case of my señorito it was suicide and nothing but suicide. To set about eating as he ate, and just after coming home in the condition he was in — that is suicide and nothing but suicide. That is what he wanted, and he had his own way!"

"Sorrows, perhaps,"

"Yes, great sorrows, very great! Women!"

"Ah! I see. But in the end there is nothing to be done but to prepare for the funeral."

Domingo was weeping.

XXXIII

W H E N I received the telegram telling me of the death of poor Augusto and learned afterwards of the circumstances attending it, I began to wonder if I had done well in saying to him what I said on that afternoon when he made me a visit to discuss with me his intention of killing himself. And I even repented of having killed him. I came to believe that he had been right, and that I ought to have let him have his own way and commit suicide. And then it occurred to me that I might bring him to life again.

"Yes," I said to myself, "I am going to bring him to life again and then let him do whatever he pleases — commit suicide, if that is his whim." And with this idea in mind of bringing him to life again I fell asleep.

Shortly after I had gone to sleep Augusto appeared to me in a dream. His figure was all white, of the whiteness of a cloud, and the outlines were illuminated as if by the rays of a setting sun. He looked at me fixedly and said to me: "I am here again."

"What have you come for?" I asked.

"To take leave of you, Don Miguel, to take leave of you for eternity; and to command you — yes, to command you — not to request you, but to command you — to write the *nivola* of my adventures."

"It is already written."

"Yes, I know, everything is written. But I am here also to tell you that this idea of yours of bringing me to life again, so that I may then, if I like, take my own life, is nonsense. What is more, it is impossible —— "

"Impossible?" I said — all this, of course, in my dream.

"Yes, impossible. That afternoon when we saw one another and talked in your study — do you remember? — and you were awake, and not sleeping and dreaming as you are now — that afternoon I told you that we who in your view are entities of fiction have a logic of our own, and that it won't work for the man who imagines us to pretend to do with us anything that may happen to suit him. Do you remember?"

"Yes, I remember."

"And although you are so very Spanish it must be perfectly clear that just now there is nothing that you desire really — isn't that so, Don Miguel?"

"Yes, I feel now no desire for anything."

"Of course not. He who sleeps and dreams has

no real desires. And you and your compatriots are
sleeping and dreaming, and you dream that you
have desires; but you don't really have them."

"You may thank God that I am sleeping," I
said to him. "For if I were not —— "

"Never mind about that. But in regard to this
matter of bringing me to life again, I am obliged
to tell you that it is not feasible. You can't do it
even if you wish to — or dream that you wish
to —— "

"But, come!"

"Yes, it is the same with an entity of fiction as
with one of flesh and bone — which you call a
man of flesh and bone and not a fiction of flesh
and bone. You can bring him into existence and
you can kill him, but once you have killed him you
cannot — no, you cannot bring him to life again.
To make a mortal and earthly man, a man of flesh
and bone who breathes the air, is easy, very easy —
unfortunately too easy. To kill a mortal and earthly
man, a man of flesh and bone who breathes the air,
is easy, very easy — unfortunately too easy. But
to bring him to life again? It is impossible to bring
him to life again."

"Quite true," I said to him. "It is impossible."

"Well, the same thing," he replied, "exactly
the same thing happens in the case of those whom
you call entities of fiction. It is easy to give us
being, perhaps too easy; and it is easy, exceedingly

easy, to kill us — perhaps only all too easy; but to bring us to life again? No one has ever really brought back to life an entity of fiction that had really died. Do you think it possible to bring Don Quixote back to life?" he asked me.

"No, it is impossible," I replied.

"Well, all the rest of us entities of fiction are in the same case."

"But what if I dream you again."

"No one dreams the same dream twice. What you will dream again and suppose to be me will be someone else. And now, now that you are asleep and dreaming and know that you are, and now that I am a dream and know that I am one — now, then, I am going to repeat to you what so greatly disturbed you when I said it before. Listen to me, my dear Don Miguel: it is quite possible that you are an entity of fiction, one who does not really exist, who is neither living nor dead. It may easily be that you are nothing more than an excuse for spreading my story through the world, and other stories like mine; and that presently, when you are dead and gone, it is we who then keep your soul alive. No, no, don't be disturbed! Although you are asleep and dreaming you are still alive now. And so, farewell!"

He evaporated into the blackish mist.

I dreamed presently that I was dying; and at

the very moment when in my dream I was taking my last breath I woke with a certain feeling of oppression in my breast.

And so this is the story of Augusto Pérez.

FUNERAL ORATION

By Way of an Epilogue

It is customary at the end of a novel, as soon as the hero or protagonist has died or married, to give an account of what happened to the rest of the characters. We shall not follow custom here; and therefore we shall give no account of what happened to Eugenia and Mauricio, to Rosario, to Liduvina and Domingo, to Don Fermín and Doña Ermelinda, to Victor and his wife, or to the others who have been introduced in connection with Augusto. Nor shall we even say what they felt and thought about the strange manner of his death. We shall make only one exception, and that will be in favor of him who felt the death of Augusto most deeply and sincerely, namely, his dog Orfeo.

Orfeo found himself an orphan. When he jumped upon the bed and, sniffing at his dead master, scented his master's death, his canine soul was enveloped in a thick, black cloud. He had experienced other deaths. He had smelt dead dogs and cats, and he had seen them; he had killed an occasional rat, and he had scented the death of men; but his master he supposed to be immortal. Because his master was for him a god. And when he saw now that he was dead he felt that within his own soul all the foundations of belief in life and the world were crumbling; and his heart was filled with an immense desolation.

And crouched at the feet of his dead master, he thought:

"Poor dear Master! Poor dear Master! He has died; he has died and left me! Everything dies, everything! Everything! Everything dies and leaves me! And it is worse to have everything die to me than for me to die to everything else. Poor dear Master! Poor dear Master! This thing that lies here, white, cold, with an odour close to putrefaction, to that of flesh to be eaten, this is no longer my master. No, it is certainly not. But where has my master gone? Where is he who used to pat me and talk to me?

"What a strange animal is man! He never seems to notice what is before him. He caresses us

and we never know why — but not when we offer
to caress him. When we devote ourselves most to
him he drives us away and beats us. There is no
way of knowing what he wants, if indeed he knows
it himself. Always he seems to be somewhere else
than where he is, and what he looks at he never
sees. It is as if there were another world for him.
And, of course, if there is another world this world
has ceased to exist.

"And then he talks, or barks, in a fashion
quite complicated. We dogs used to howl, but to
please him we learned to bark. Yet even so we don't
come to an understanding with him. We only really
understand him when he also howls. When a man
howls or shouts or threatens, we other animals understand him very well! Then his attention is not
in that other world! But he barks in a way all his
own — he speaks. And this has enabled him to invent what does not exist and to overlook what exists. As soon as he gives a thing a name he ceases
to see the thing itself; he only hears the name that
he gave it or sees it written. His language enables
him to falsify, to ,invent what does not exist, and
to confuse himself. For him everything in the world
is merely a pretext for talking to other men or for

talking to himself. Yes, he has even infected us dogs with this!

"*He is a sick animal, there's no doubt about that. He is always sick! Only when he is asleep does he seem to enjoy any measure of health, and not always then; for there are times when he even talks in his sleep! And he has infected us with this too. He has infected us with so many things!*

"*And then he insults us! He gives the name of cynicism, which means caninism, or doggishness, to impudence and shamelessness — he who is really of all animals the most shameless and hypocritical! His language has made him a hypocrite. So that, if shamelessness is to be named cynicism, then by the same token hypocrisy should be named anthropism, or humanism.*

"*And he wants to make us hypocrites too! He wants us dogs to play the part of clowns and buffoons! Us dogs, who were never conquered and tamed by him, like the bull or the horse, by force, but who joined ourselves to him freely, in a mutual agreement for the pursuit of game. We discovered the game for him, he gave chase, and then he gave us our part. And thus our partnership began in a social contract.*

"And now he has rewarded us by insulting us and debasing us, trying to make us into clowns and apes and wise dogs! "Wise dogs" *is the name that these men give to the performing dogs they teach to act; for which purpose they put clothes upon them and teach them to walk on their hind legs, most indecorously. Wise dogs! This is what men call wisdom — to act a part and walk upon two legs!*

"Of course a dog that walks upon his hind legs exhibits the private parts of his body shamelessly and self-consciously. This is what happened to man when he rose upon his feet and turned himself into an upright mammal. At once he had a feeling of shame and felt it necessary to cover the parts that he was showing. And for this reason his Bible says, as I have heard from men, that the first man — that is to say, the first who undertook to walk upon his hind legs — was ashamed to present himself naked before his God. And for this reason they invented clothes, to cover up their sex. But since both sexes began by wearing the same garments they did not always distinguish one sex from the other, and this gave rise to a thousand evils — peculiarly human atrocities which they are at pains

to call cur-like or cynical. It is they, the men, who have perverted us, the dogs. It is they who have made us cur-like and cynical. This is the hypocrisy in us. For cynicism in a dog is hypocrisy just as hypocrisy in a man is cynicism. Each of us has infected the other.

"When men put on clothes it was at first the same garments for men and women. But when the sexes thus became confused they had to invent different garments and put sex into clothes. These trousers are simply the result of man's having undertaken to walk upon two feet.

"What a strange animal is man! His mind is never where it ought to be, namely, where he is himself; he talks in order to lie; and he wears clothes!

"Poor Master! Within a short time they will bury him in a place set apart for the purpose. Men preserve and store up their dead, and they refuse to allow the dogs and the crows to eat them! To what purpose? That there may be left of them at last only what every animal, beginning with man himself, leaves in the world, namely, a few bones. They store up their dead! An animal that speaks, wears clothes, and stores up his dead! Poor man!

"*Poor dear Master! Poor dear Master! He was a man; yes, he was not more than a man; he was only a man! But he was my master! And without ever knowing it, how much he owed to me! — how much! How much I taught him by my silences, and by licking his hands while he kept talking and talking and talking to me. 'Will you understand me?' he used to say to me. Oh, yes! I understood him. I understood him all the while he was talking and talking and talking. In talking to me, thus talking to himself, he talked to the dog that was in him. I kept his cynicism awake.*

"*It was a dog's life that he led, a perfect dog's life! And it was a monstrous dog's trick, or rather a monstrous human trick, that those two played him! A man's trick that Mauricio played him, a woman's trick that Eugenia played him. Poor dear Master!*

"*And now you lie here, cold, white, motionless, clothed indeed but without the power of speech either for talking to others or for talking to yourself. And you have nothing to say to poor Orfeo. Neither can Orfeo tell you anything by his silence.*

"*Poor dear Master! What can have become of*

*him? Where can that part of him be which spoke
and dreamed in him? Perhaps there above, in the
pure world, on the high plateau of the earth, in that
fine region of the earth, all of it in fine colours as
Plato saw it, which men call divine; upon that ter-
restrial plane from which the precious stones fall,
where the pure men dwell, and the purified, drinking the air and breathing the ether. There also are
the purified dogs, the dogs of San Humberto the
hunter, and the dog of Santo Domingo de Guzmán
with his torch in his mouth; of San Roque, of
whom a preacher used to say, pointing to an image
of him, 'Here you have San Roque, dog and all!'
There in that pure Platonic world, in that world of
incarnate ideas, lives the pure dog, the dog that is
in the true sense cynical. And there too dwells my
master!*

*"I feel my own soul becoming purified by this
contact with death, with this purification of my
master. I feel it mounting upward towards the mist
into which he at last was dissolved, the mist from
which he sprang and to which he returned. Orfeo
feels the dark mist coming. And he runs to his master, jumping and wagging his tail. Dear Master!
Dear Master! Poor man!"*

A little later Domingo and Liduvina picked up the poor dog lying dead at the feet of his master, like him purified, and enveloped like him in the dark cloud. And when poor Domingo saw that, he was deeply affected and he wept. Whether for the death of his master or for the death of the dog, it might be hard to say. But it is most likely that he wept at the sight of that marvellous example of faithfulness and loyalty. And he exclaimed:

"And yet they say that grief never kills!"